How to Run Your Department Successfully

Related titles

How to be a Successful Form Tutor – Michael Marland and
 Rick Rogers

How to Run Your School Successfully – Adrian Percival and
 Susan Tranter

How to Run Your Department Successfully

Chris Turner

continuum
LONDON • NEW YORK

Continuum International Publishing Group
The Tower Building   15 East 26th Street
11 York Road   New York, NY 10010
London
SE1 7NX

                www.continuumbooks.com

British Library Cataloguing-in-Publication Data
A catalogue record for this book is available from the British Library.

ISBN: 0 8264 7040 8 (hardback) 0 8264 7041 6 (paperback)

Library of Congress Cataloging-in-Publication Data
A catalog record for this book is available from the Library of Congress.

Typeset by Aarontype Limited, Easton, Bristol
Printed and bound in Great Britain by MPG Books Ltd, Bodmin, Cornwall

Contents

Acknowledgements

I wish to express my thanks to all those who helped in the compilation of the material for this book, especially Professor Ray Bolam whose advice and encouragement have sustained me in the last ten years; to the staff working in the secondary schools in England and Wales who allowed me to interview them about their work; to the Headteachers of 'Central' School, 'Highway' School and 'Woodland' School for giving me every assistance in the research required for Phase 3; to my colleagues in the ex-Education Department of the University of Wales, Swansea (now known as the Swansea School of Education) especially Dr John Parkinson and Nigel Norman for their help and encouragement. Finally, I wish to thank all the staff at Continuum for their support, especially Alexandra Webster and Christina Parkinson.

This book is dedicated to my family, especially my sons Ben, Sam and Jack.

I am very grateful to Taylor and Francis for giving me permission to include two chapters in this book which were originally published in the journal entitled 'School Leadership and Management'. The two chapters appear in this book in a revised form to take account of new ideas which have emerged since they were originally published.

Chapter 8 'Managing a subject' was first published as:

Turner, C.K. (2003) 'The distinctiveness of the subject being taught and the work of subject heads of department in managing the quality of classroom teaching and learning in secondary schools in Wales', *School Leadership and Management*, 23, 1, p. 41–58.

Chapter 9 'Learning from Experience' was first published as:

Turner, C.K. (2000) 'Learning about leading a subject department in secondary schools: some empirical evidence', *School Leadership and Management*, 20, 3, p. 299–314.

For further details please see the journal website:

www.tandf.co.uk/journals

1 Subject leaders: policy and practice

Introduction

The contents of this book are based on work carried out in the last ten years among subject leaders (SLs) working in secondary schools. The motivation arose partly from a conviction that SLs were a vital element in the drive to raise standards and bring about school improvement and partly from a personal standpoint, as I was interested in reflecting upon and analysing my own work as an SL. I had held the post of Head of Physics for six years in a secondary school in North Kent and had also been a Head of Faculty as Head of Science in another secondary school in Kent. Successful subject leaders work closely with other members of their department to provide inspiring leadership and galvanize their colleagues to utilize their talents to the full. However, their work is framed in an over-arching educational policy context which is described in this chapter.

It should be noted that the terms 'subject leader' and 'Head of Department' (HoD) are used interchangeably throughout this book. It is recognized that the leadership element is the vital factor (for example, in providing the necessary enthusiasm and motivating others) in bringing about improvements in teaching and learning in the subject. The title 'HoD' is an administrative one which denotes a post of responsibility for managing the performance of pupils in a given subject.

Background to the research

The evidence referred to in this book has been collected in three distinct phases. The main aim of the investigation has been to find out more about how HoDs bring about improvements in teaching and learning in their subject. Thus the underlying assumption in this book is that HoDs who run their departments successfully are able to bring about these improvements.

Phase 1

A survey was carried out among SLs in four subject areas in Wales; namely in Science, English, Mathematics and Technology. The first three were chosen because they are core subjects and Technology was selected because it was a foundation subject but comparable in size, as far as staffing is concerned, to the other three major subject departments in most secondary schools. More details about the sample used in the Phase 1 research can be found in Appendix 1.

Phase 2

As a follow-up to the work done in Phase 1, it was decided to obtain more information about how HoDs influenced teaching and learning. Semi-structured interviews were undertaken with a total of thirty-six HoDs who had already participated in Phase 1. They worked in ten secondary schools situated in different locations in Wales in a research project funded by the ESRC (No.R000221971). More details about Phase 2 of the research can be found in Appendix 2.

Phase 3

Interviews were carried out with subject HoDs and their line managers in three secondary schools in different parts of England (namely Highway, Central and Woodland). The people interviewed were selected on the basis of recommendations made by the appropriate member of the Senior Management Team (SMT) in their schools, on the basis of being successful practitioners. The main aim of Phase 3 was to provide insights on the work of HoDs in the light of current educational policy in regard to performance management, management of pupil data and the introduction of the Key Stage 3 policy in England. Further details of the Phase 3 sample can be found in Appendix 3.

Definitions of leadership and management

The working definitions for leadership and management to be used in this book are outlined below.

Educational leadership is primarily concerned with policy formulation and organizational transformation (Bolam, 1999). It is within this context that I would like to define leadership in two ways: 1. following Stogdill (1950) as: 'the process of influencing the activities of an organised group toward goal setting and goal achievement' (p. 3). Thus the leader is perceived to be influencing the behaviour of the group in the direction of desired goals; and 2. following Greenfield (1986): 'leadership is a wilful act where one person attempts to construct the social world for others' (p. 142). Bryman (1999) referred to this aspect as the leader being the 'manager of meaning', which may be interpreted as attempting to make sense of events and building a social consensus around the interpretations. The leader is playing a very important part in defining the organizational reality for and with others. Bryman (1999) criticized the notion of influence as implying a one-way leadership process and he justified the use of the phrase 'manager of meaning' by arguing that: 'the focus of meaning might be taken to imply that a wider constituency of organisational members are implicated in leadership' (p. 27).

In my opinion, in the context of the work of HoDs, the notion of social influence is particularly relevant, since most, if not all, members of a subject department can have the opportunity to influence group thinking, in formal and informal settings. The two-way nature of influence was noted by Luthans (1998) when he commented that there was evidence that:

> subordinates affect leaders and their behaviours as much as leaders and their behaviours affect subordinates. (p. 386)

Educational management can be distinguished from educational leadership in the sense that it is an executive function dedicated to the implementation of agreed policy (following Bolam, 1999). According to Bolman and Deal (1994), management deals with maintaining the status quo. It is interested in the operation of the system as it is currently constructed, and is preoccupied with 'firefighting'. A useful addition to the understanding of management may be gleaned from Mintzberg (1990) who argued from a business perspective that managers will undertake three different roles in the area of interpersonal relationships, which are derived from their formally delegated authority. These roles may be reinterpreted to suit the educational context of this study, as:

- a *figurehead*, which may more correctly be described as an HoD acting as a role model, particularly in his/her willingness to embrace and adapt to change
- a *leader*, which might be more appropriately described as a team leader, since the quality of teamwork and collegial practice which is achieved in the department, is vital to its success as well as being pro-active in the area of professional development
- a manager who *liaises* with others, which is crucially important for HoDs, as a great deal of their work involves communicating and taking decisions with members of the department, other HoDs and with members of the Senior Management Team (SMT), not to mention non-teaching staff, governors, parents and pupils. This liaison role also involves monitoring the quality of the departmental work

One important distinction between management and leadership is the debate concerning two role functions, normally applied to headteachers: 'leading professional' and 'chief executive', first explored by Hughes (1987). In their research with primary headteachers, Bell and Bawden (2000) found that increasing demands on both functions meant that neither aspect was being given the attention it deserved. The chief executive role was described as being acted out in the context of: 'performance management, arrangements for accountability, and the monitoring of pupil achievement' (p. 15). At the same time, the leading professional role placed great emphasis on:

> establishing a vision for the school, achieving National Standards and implementing the next phase of the National Curriculum. (p. 15)

In a similar fashion, subject leaders in secondary schools fulfil many of the same executive and leading professional functions, as can be seen in Table 1.1. This comparison mainly draws upon the original idea taken from Hughes (1987), who suggested that both functions have internal (i.e. within the school) and external dimensions. Both of these roles are important when considering the work of subject leaders and need to be fulfilled at the same time, whilst recognizing that each may be treated separately.

Table 1.1   A comparison of the leading professional and executive roles of subject leaders

Leading professional	Executive
Internal Professional guidance in terms of curriculum planning; sharing good practice; pioneering new ideas; suggesting courses for departmental staff to attend; exemplar of high standards of teaching (acting as a role model).	**Internal** Allocating staff to classes; allocating resources; coordinator; monitor of standards; delegator of responsibilities to others in the department.
External Acting as spokesperson for the department in meetings with SMT, parents and governors.	**External** Developing and maintaining good working relationships with other HoDs, SMT, LEA personnel, and governors.

Educational policy and the work of subject leaders

The three most relevant policy innovations in the last six years have been:

- the Teacher Training Agency (TTA, 1998) standards for subject leaders working in schools in England and Wales
- the introduction of performance management in 2000 in schools in England which currently provide an important working context for subject leaders, and
- the introduction of the KS3 Strategy in 2001 which was seen by policy-makers as a way of raising standards

The TTA standards

In the latter part of the 1990s, policy-makers began to realize that a new breed of leader was required at middle management level in secondary schools to cope with the increasing burden of responsibilities which were being devolved by Headteachers to post-holders such as Heads of Department. The TTA produced a document in 1998 called *National Standards for Subject Leaders*. Its main aim was to define expertise in a key role such as a subject leader and to:

help teachers at different points in the profession to plan and monitor their development, training and performance effectively and to set clear and relevant targets for improving their effectiveness. (p. 1)

The TTA (1998) document stated what it considered the main task areas, which HoDs need to tackle. They are:

(a) Providing strategic direction and development of the subject
(b) Managing teaching and learning
(c) Leading and managing staff
(d) The effective deployment of staff and resources

In addition, the standards describe the kinds of knowledge, skills and attitudes which may be desirable in HoDs. These are conceived as generic and therefore take no account of the type of department being led and managed. In small departments, for example, there is little opportunity for delegation. In addition, the range of tasks to be covered inevitably lead, in my view, to some form of task prioritization on a day-by-day basis.

A major area of change is in the performance management aspects of an HoD's work, which were referred to in the TTA standards in section B (vii) as:

set expectations and targets for staff and pupils in relation to standards of pupils' achievement and the quality of teaching; set clear targets for pupil achievement, and evaluate progress and achievement in the subject by all pupils, including those with special educational and linguistic needs. (TTA, 1998, p. 11)

Taking time to examine all the aspects of the task areas described in the TTA (1998) document would quickly lead any interested reader to conclude that it would be impossible for any HoD, however dedicated, to accomplish all the stated tasks. Some form of prioritization is essential. Wise and Bush (1999) reported the findings from a postal survey of two hundred and twenty-two middle managers in two LEAs. As part of this work, the respondents were asked to place twelve tasks in priority order. Among the most notable results from this work was the relatively high ranking given to 'supervising/monitoring colleagues' work to ensure that policies are followed through' (p. 190). This task was ranked fourth, with teaching the subject, developing the curriculum and implementing school policy being the three top priorities. This finding contrasts with the pre-1988 work done by Earley and Fletcher-Campbell (1992), who noted that many HoDs did not accept the responsibility for monitoring and evaluating the work of their colleagues. It therefore now appears that HoDs have indeed accepted more responsibility for the managerial tasks, possibly as a result of the all-pervasive policy climate of school improvement and performance management.

Performance management (PM)

In England, as a result of amendments to the Appraisal regulations originally brought in in 1992, new PM arrangements came into force in September 2000 (DfEE, 2000) and in Wales in September 2002. The responsibility for the strategic implementation of these regulations was devolved to governors. In Wales, very similar regulations have been more recently introduced by the Welsh Assembly for PM in November 2002.

A budget of £20 million was set aside in 2000–1 for the relevant training in PM. A further £20 million was available from 2001 to help schools operate the new performance review arrangement in England. However, this was not the case in Wales where schools did not have any additional funding made available.

The DfEE (2000) document advocates PM on the basis of five principles: equity; raising standards; continuous professional development (CPD); involvement and manageability. Schools which have already acquired the Investors in People quality kitemark may well find that little adaptation would be needed for the introduction of PM. PM is based on a three-stage cycle involving planning, monitoring and review. Planning could involve the setting of between three and six objectives for one year. An individual Action Plan can then be drawn up to show how the teacher intends to meet these objectives. It should be agreed with the team leader. Monitoring involves an annual lesson observation with feedback (as a minimum) from the line manager. Review of performance can take the form of an evaluation and identification of CPD needs.

The designers of the framework advocated five principles which underpin PM policy: namely, raising standards (allied to current government policy); continuous professional development (which may well appeal to teachers trying to adjust to a rapidly changing world where new technology is increasingly playing an important part); involvement, mainly in whole-school planning (which addresses the concerns of some staff who may have felt disenfranchised in the decision-making process); manageability, to encourage more 'joined-up' thinking in terms of the minds of teachers, particularly in relation to threshold payments and target-setting policies; and finally equity, which is founded on openness and fair play while respecting confidentiality.

The PM cycle is envisaged to be an annual process and consists of three stages.

Stage 1   Planning: whole-school policy would determine the number and nature of the objectives to be set. One objective would commonly relate to a target concerning pupil performance.

Stage 2   Monitoring: progress is monitored by a mixture of informal discussion and classroom observation. The lesson observation would be followed by constructive feedback by the team leader. This is a process with which recent entrants to the profession are very familiar. Perhaps the most important aspect of monitoring is the discussion concerning the specific areas being focused on, for example, the management of pupil behaviour or whether the learning objectives for the lesson were achieved.

Stage 3   Yearly review: the outcomes of this process may well be very important to the career of the individual teacher, because it may decide whether that teacher is awarded an incremental pay award. However, this presupposes that the school budget has been set at a level which sustains such an award or awards.

The individual teacher has his/her performance reviewed by a team leader. In a department, that would normally be the HoD but in many large departments, other staff such the second-in-department would be employed as a team leader. No one team leader would normally be placed in charge of more than four members of staff.

PM has a number of implications for subject leaders. Team leaders (such as HoDs) are charged with the responsibility of implementing performance management in England and Wales at departmental level. Its advocates (for example, Hartle *et al.*, 2001, p. 53) argue that team leaders are expected to:

- help teachers to identify objectives and create an improvement plan
- challenge and support teachers and ensure alignment of personal objectives with department and school targets
- provide guidance, coaching and support to help others improve their performance
- provide regular timely and constructive feedback
- make objective judgements about performance

Four major areas of difficulty may cause problems for HoDs. Firstly, there may be disagreement between the team leader and an individual member of the department over what constitutes a 'good' lesson. This could potentially cause damage to collegial relationships within the department (referred to by Arrowsmith, 2001). Secondly, damage to morale may also occur if the training needs identified by a performance review are not met satisfactorily. Thirdly, it should not be assumed that all teachers are filled with the same desire to improve the quality of their teaching. More experienced staff who have been passed over for promotion may lack the motivation to address any shortcomings in their own teaching seriously. Fourthly, team leaders are themselves busy teachers and it may well be extremely challenging for HoDs to find the time to provide the necessary support and coaching to help others improve their performance.

The team leader would normally be the HoD. What is clear is how an individual teacher might expect to benefit from this exercise. It should bring out targets for CPD and the opportunity to have a professional discussion about their work and an assessment of their performance. However, dealing with weak or under-performance is likely to be much more problematic for the team leader. It could seriously damage departmental relationships on which so much depends. It is not so obvious as to how PM will benefit pupils and it is likely to be some time before any judgements can be made about its effects on pupil learning.

The Key Stage 3 strategy

The reasons why the strategy was needed were set out on the Standards Site' (DfES, 2001). The main argument advocated by the policy-makers appeared to centre on the rising levels of pupil attainment at the end of KS2. Significant rises in both literacy and numeracy scores in the period between 1998 and 2000 were cited, along with the desire to see achievement levels rising at the end of KS3. The DfES document outlines four major areas of concern in KS3:

- a perceived dip in the performance of pupils at the start of secondary education
- concern about the various forms of disaffection shown by some pupils in KS3
- inspection evidence raising questions about the quality of teaching in KS3 and
- a slower than expected rate of progress between the ages of 11 and 14 for many pupil (particularly in relation to boys' underachievement)

The Strategy consists of a number of different components: 'booster' lessons which can be taught in Year 9 prior to the sitting of the National Tests; catch-up classes in Year 7 aimed at helping those pupils who did not achieve level 4 in KS2; summer schools for pupils to attend offering help with literacy and numeracy where it is needed; more training opportunities for staff to find out more about the latest ideas on assessment for learning, developing thinking skills and understanding more about pupils' preferred learning styles in relation to Gardner's (1993) theories about multiple intelligences. In addition, a series of very challenging targets were set, namely:

- ✓ by 2004, 75 per cent of all 14 year olds would achieve level 5 in English, Maths and ICT and 70 per cent in Science
- ✓ by 2007, 85 per cent will achieve level 5 in English, Maths and ICT and 80 per cent in Science
- ✓ by 2004, no LEA would achieve less than 65 per cent at level 5 and above in English and Maths and 60 per cent in Science

These targets are very ambitious and rely on very careful monitoring of progress during Key Stage 3. More details of the issues involved in the successful management of the strategy can be found in Chapter 12.

Structure of this book

Following this chapter, the next two set out the principles which underpin the work of subject leaders. It is very difficult to discuss the concept of subject leadership in isolation from subject departments, as it is the department which provides a working context for the exercise of leadership. Thus Chapter 2 attempts to deal with leadership from a variety of relevant up-to-date perspectives as well as outlining details of our current state of knowledge in relation to subject departments. Chapter 3 provides an overview of the tasks to be addressed by subject leaders, using the TTA (1998) standards as a focus for the discussion. In addition, an outline of what we know from research about the methods or strategies which subject leaders use, is then included.

Chapters 4–9 attempt to combine the research findings from Phases 1 and 2 with issues of practical importance to subject leaders. A great deal has been written in the past about the importance of teamwork and Chapter 4 focuses on the role of the subject leader as a team leader. Chapter 5 presents a picture of subject leaders managing their staff from a political standpoint, drawing on the research carried out in Phase 2. Negotiation, bargaining and conflict may well be part and parcel of an HoD's work, although these micropolitical processes usually place a heavy reliance on the goodwill of departmental staff. Chapter 6 argues that subject leaders can be equally concerned with the initiation and implementation of change.

Departmental planning is an important aspect of a subject leader's work, which is framed in a whole-school context. Chapter 7 explores the links between strategic planning, whole-school action planning and departmental planning. It tries to explain these links by way of examples taken from practice. Chapter 8 focuses on four different curriculum subjects (three core and one foundation) and attempts to distinguish their unique features, as well as discussing the implications of these differences in terms of leading and managing the subject. Chapter 9 is derived mainly from research done in Phase 2 where HoDs were asked to discuss how they were able to manage their departments well with relatively little formalized training for the role of HoD. The key ideas included here are organizational and professional socialization, which appear to play a major part in the professional development of the staff involved.

Chapters 10, 11 and 12 place a particular emphasis on the findings from Phase 3 of the research for this book. Chapter 10 discusses one of the more neglected areas (in terms of published literature) of a subject leader's work, namely, their part in helping to shape the professional development of departmental staff. It is one thing to collect vast amounts of data on pupil achievements, but it is something else to use it intelligently as a means of monitoring pupil progress. Chapter 11 deals with the management of pupil performance in terms of tracking pupil progress and the variety of ways in which subject leaders use data in their specific curriculum areas. Chapter 12 relates to the management of the Key Stage 3 strategy by HoDs.

The final chapter, Chapter 13, attempts to provide an overview of the work done by subject leaders in terms of describing the work they do to contribute to the 'bigger picture'. Schools are in the business of helping young people develop their full potential in terms of the knowledge, understanding and skills necessary to cope with the rapidly changing world of the twenty-first century.

Owing to the limitations of space, this book does not attempt to cover every aspect of the successful operation of a department. The topics which have been selected for discussion and analysis try to represent the work of subject leaders in the twenty-first century, as it is experienced by HoDs in a modern educational policy context. Those aspects not covered include curriculum issues and preferred learning styles; working with the departmental staff in order to provide SEN pupils with the best possible educational opportunities; working with support staff, which, in some subject areas, is a really vital part of the role of the subject leader (e.g. in Science); and finally, cross-curricular and extra-curricular work.

Discussion points
1. Following the introduction of Performance Management in schools in England and Wales, what would you say are its significant advantages and disadvantages:
   (a) from your personal perspective as an existing or aspiring subject leader?
   (b) from the subject department perspective?

2. To what extent has the implementation of the Key Stage 3 strategy had an impact in your subject area, in terms of:
   (a) teaching and learning
   (b) leading and managing the department
   (c) professional development of the department staff?
3. To what extent do you, as an existing or aspiring HoD, agree/disagree with the functional distinctions which have been drawn between being a leading professional and an executive, as described in Table 1.1?
4. 'HoDs shoulder all the responsibility for pupils' performance in the subject but exercise very little formal authority.' To what extent do you agree/disagree with this statement?
5. Based on the working definitions of leadership and management given in this chapter, it would be more important for a headteacher to be a leader rather than a manager. To what extent do you think that is also true for HoDs?

Further reading

Blanchard, J. (2002) *Teaching and Targets: Self-Evaluation and School Improvement*, London: RoutledgeFalmer.

Gleeson, D. and Husbands, C. (eds) (2001) *The Performing School*, London: RoutledgeFalmer.

Ofsted/DfEE (1996) *Setting Targets to Raise Standards: A Survey of Good Practice*, London: Ofsted.

Ruding, E. (2000) *Middle Management in Action: Practical Approaches to School Improvement*, London: RoutledgeFalmer.

Yukl, G. (1994) *Leadership in Organisations* (3rd edn), Englewood Cliffs, NJ: Prentice-Hall.

2 Subject leadership and subject departments

Introduction

This chapter attempts to outline current thinking on leadership as it might apply to HoDs and subject departments, which are a common feature of secondary schools in the UK. The principles discussed here will be applied in subsequent chapters when appropriate.

Ideas about leadership

Seven perspectives on leadership are discussed in this section. They reflect its multi-dimensional nature and all are relevant to the ways in which HoDs exercise leadership.

Situational leadership

This reflects the contingent nature of schools and departments and the different contexts in which they operate. If all the teaching of a given subject is concentrated in a specified area of the school, the task of leading such a department is very different, compared to coping in a subject where the teaching is taking place in different parts of the school and the staff do not have regular contact with each other. Thinking about the role of the HoD from a situational perspective places an emphasis on the fact that there is no one right way to lead and manage. Schools and departments vary considerably in size and in character. The variation at department level can also be illustrated by comparing the managerial approach adopted by a relatively inexperienced subject leader in a Mathematics department full of experienced staff to that of a more experienced subject leader in an English department, dominated by newly qualified staff. Thus the ways in which leadership is exercised are contingent upon the situation in

which the subject leader finds him/herself. According to Yukl
(1994), situational leadership:

> emphasises the importance of contextual factors, such as the nature
> of the work performed [in the subject department], the nature of
> the external environment and the characteristics of the followers
> [the departmental staff]. (p. 13)

According to Hersey *et al.* (1996), situational leadership matches
leadership style to the working context and the three most important aspects are:

- the kinds of demands the job makes on leadership
- the nature and distribution of power and authority
- the expectations of other people with whom the leader works

They commented on the important part played by followers
(departmental colleagues in this context) when discussing this form
of leadership. This is because the departmental staff can actually
determine the extent to which they are willing to be influenced by
the HoD. This assumes that the department represents the major
arena of influence for a subject leader and, generally speaking, the
prevailing ethos is a collegial one.

Hersey *et al.* (1996) identified an additional concept which they
called 'readiness'. This is associated with two components: *willingness*, which they define as 'the extent to which an individual has the
confidence, commitment and motivation to accomplish a specific
task' (p. 195) and *ability*, which is the knowledge, experience and
skill that an individual brings to a task. They argued that these con-
cepts are not discrete but interacting. The subject leader therefore
needs to make a judgement about the willingness and ability of
each of his/her colleagues, when deliberating whether a task is
likely to be successfully completed. Therefore, if a member of the
departmental team becomes more willing to achieve a particular
task, then he/she will use his/her ability more effectively.

Transformational leadership
Transformational leadership incorporates the crucial element of
vision-building and vision-sharing within the departmental team
(Starratt, 1995). Burns (1978) commented on the importance of

transformational leadership, because it placed the emphasis on out-comes as well as processes. Subject leaders play an important part in improving standards of teaching and learning. This may well involve the HoD challenging existing attitudes among departmental staff towards, for example, pupil attainment, monitoring and per-formance management. However, at a fundamental level, transfor-mational leadership is about building and sharing a vision of the characteristics of high-quality teaching and learning with the subject teaching staff and how that vision might be realized.

In Bolam and Turner's (1999) research, most of the HoDs inter-viewed appeared to agree with the notion that they had to be capable of sharing their vision about teaching the subject. One interviewee made an important response: 'sharing the vision is important, but having the vision in the first place is even more important' (p. 254). This research also pointed out the necessity for HoDs to listen to the opinions of the departmental staff and value their contributions. Sharing of professional knowledge in departmental meetings was seen as a very important aspect of improving classroom practice. Brown *et al.* (2000) noted that decisions were often made without any real consultation and this led to a feeling that whatever 'vision' existed tended to be 'handed down'. HoDs felt that their contribu-tion to the vision-building process was often undervalued by the SMT and governors.

Moral leadership
This perspective on leadership can involve the HoD superimposing the values which are important to him/her on to colleagues, when exercising leadership. Hodgkinson (1991) argued that:

> the educational leader is caught in a field of values in which he is forced to choose and act. (p. 43)

As Figure 2.1 illustrates, the central value is that of the self-interest of the individual (V1). However, the informal group with which he/she works, i.e. the department, sets out its own values (V2), which may in some ways be at odds with those of the whole-school or organizational culture (V3). For example, the SMT would like to see the adoption of a rigid setting policy across the board from Year 7, which certain departments might strongly oppose.

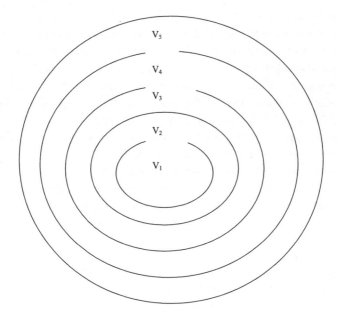

V1   Personal values of individual staff
V2   Group (departmental) values – concerned with roles, tasks, goals, policies and purposes
V3   School values at an organizational level – concerned with roles, tasks, goals, policies and purposes
V4   Local community values shaped by LEA, parents, employers, etc.
V5   National values incorporating the cultural 'spirit of the times' (Zeitgeist)

Figure 2.1   Values operating at different levels within the education system in a departmental context

No school exists outside the community it serves and it may be that the local community values (V4), whose expectations of the educational process are traditionally very low, do not match those of the school which is trying to achieve higher standards. V5 represents, in Hodgkinson's view, the Zeitgeist or prevailing attitudes towards education which may, for example, put a great deal of value on equality of opportunity. At any given moment of time, all of these values are competing for adoption in the hearts and minds of staff, parents and pupils.

Political leadership

Political leadership includes notions of the exercise of power in terms of both influence and authority. Subject leaders have very little formalized authority in the way that a headteacher does. However, they can exercise influence in various ways within the subject area. For example, Bolman and Deal (1994) argued that political leadership can build 'supportive coalitions and alliances to make desirable things happen' (p. 83). This perspective also includes *transactional leadership* (Burns, 1978), which emphasized negotiation between the leader and the followers (very important in the day-to-day work of HoDs), as well as leaders gaining compliance by offering rewards and/or punishments. The study of political dealings inside an organization is called micropolitics. According to Hoyle (1986), micropolitics consists

> of the strategies by which individuals and groups in organisational contexts seek to use their resources of *authority* and *influence* to further their interests. (p. 126)

The emphasis (*italics*) is mine, since, in my opinion, these represent the most important elements of micropolitics as applied to HoDs. The *authority* of a subject leader is founded on three principles:

- the status which may be associated with the post of responsibility; (for example, the post of Head of Mathematics or Head of English in any secondary school is a high-status position)
- the acknowledged expertise of the subject leader in teaching the subject, which is reflected in good examination results achieved by pupils
- credibility acquired by the subject leader while in post, where the respect of colleagues is earned over time

The *influence* exerted by a subject leader can occur in two ways: through informal contact with departmental colleagues, and in more formal contexts such as staff meetings or departmental meetings. One example of the work of a subject leader from a political perspective can be seen in the need for the HoD to monitor and evaluate the work of their colleagues, which could potentially conflict with notions of professional autonomy. The result of such monitoring runs the risk of damaging professional relationships between colleagues in departments. Earley and Fletcher-Campbell (1992) discussed the problems faced by HoDs in monitoring and evaluating the work of their departmental colleagues effectively, since any form of classroom observation of subject staff can conflict with notions of professional autonomy as well as being

> frequently associated with accountability and often thought of in terms of weeding out the inefficient and dismissing incompetent teachers. (p. 117)

Glover *et al.* (1999a) found that there was some reluctance on the part of subject leaders to embrace their responsibilities to monitor and evaluate performance, because they felt that professional relationships with colleagues may be compromised. For example, according to one deputy head, 'some subject leaders retreat into administration so they can plead that they have not got time to undertake additional duties' (p. 341). One HoD in this study considered that this reluctance was justified because he did not consider himself to be the best teacher in the department. However, with the adoption of performance management, it is likely that SLs will engage in monitoring and evaluation on a more regular basis.

Paradoxically, Earley and Fletcher-Campbell (1992) noted that, if HoDs were able to develop the ability to be able to 'helicopter' (i.e. take a whole-school perspective), then they would be more highly regarded by senior staff in schools. By way of contrast:

> Middle managers who fought for their own corner regardless of the needs of colleagues in other departments and whole school policies were regarded unfavourably. (p. 196)

Yet, departmental staff expect their HoD to represent their views to the Headteacher and SMT. The liaison role thus presents HoDs with a challenging task and requires that they develop the skills of a political leader. More on the micropolitical aspects of a subject leader's work can be found in Chapter 5.

Symbolic leadership
This form of leadership is perhaps most applicable when the HoD is acting as a role model for other less experienced members of the

department. The symbolic nature of leadership emphasizes the critical importance of culture, values and vision. Leaders should communicate some form of vision but it cannot be imposed on reluctant followers. There is a need to engage people in the process of vision building, which can be associated with the use of symbols. A simple example of this might be the desire to value the pupils' work in a more explicit and symbolic way, by the use of certificates which commend pupils for their efforts or the display of pupils' work as exemplars of good practice.

Distributed leadership

A more recent conceptualization of leadership involves a move away from considering the HoD as a heroic and charismatic figure, leading the department from the front while their colleagues dutifully follow. This is what Gronn (2000) referred to as a 'naive realism', a belief that only one person can exercise leadership. Instead, it becomes distributed among all those who work in the department so that all the required tasks can be accomplished as a result of collaborative effort. In other words, the nominated subject leader may not be doing all the leading. If it is accepted that leadership is a form of social influence, then different members of the department can exert great influence in particular contexts. One of the most obvious examples of this is where one departmental colleague demonstrates some aspect of the use of ICT to the rest of the department on a training day in school.

Team leadership

As I have already stated, the extent to which a leader can influence the quality of the work done in their department partly depends on the context: i.e. the size of the department, the status of the subject within the school, and the experience of the team members. Where the subject leader has line-management responsibility for a number of departmental colleagues, then achieving desired goals becomes a high priority. This will only occur when all the team members are working towards the same agreed goals; for example, high standards of teaching and learning in the subject. Much of the time, this will involve formal and informal discussion in meetings and can present the team leader with a variety of challenges. For example, if the subject leader is relatively inexperienced as a Head of Department and the department contains a number of long-standing staff, then he/she may find a great deal of resistance to any suggested change in departmental practice.

According to Bolam and Turner (1999), when HoDs were asked about how they promoted good teaching and learning in practice, the most popular response was to hold regular meetings (especially by Heads of English). Formal or informal contact with departmental staff can serve to bring about improvements in classroom practice, as long as the leader (HoD) is able to provide the necessary transformational leadership required. Aspects of team leadership are discussed in more detail in Chapter 4.

Gender and subject leadership

Does gender make a difference when considering the work of HoDs? Most of the published work dealing with gender issues and leadership has been directed towards headteachers (Hall, 1996), or other senior managers in education (Shakeshaft, 1987). According to Adler et al. (1993), research in educational management makes the assumption that:

> the experiences of males and females are the same and therefore research on males is appropriate for generalising the female experience. Female experiences are ignored or diminished. (p. 6)

This androcentric view has been strongly challenged by Shakeshaft (1987) and Hall (1999) who argued for:

> a more integrated analysis of gender and management that recognises . . . the diversity of masculinities and feminities that characterise managers' behaviour. (p. 160)

Therefore, it may well be that female subject leaders bring certain qualities to the post of subject leader which are not so prevalent among male subject leaders, but there is insufficient research evidence at the present time to know precisely what they might be.

Subject leaders and the use of non-contact time

Most subject leaders have a limited number of 'free' periods or non-contact time. They would be expected to use this time to do their administration and accomplish many of the tasks outlined in Chapter 3. As long ago as 1992, Earley and Fletcher-Campbell recommended that more non-contact time be made available for HoDs to perform their tasks effectively, particularly in the key area of being able to visit the classrooms of members of departmental staff (and offer reciprocal opportunities) and exchange ideas in a non-threatening way.

Glover and Miller (1999b) were interested in determining to what extent HoDs were able to deal with the current demands on their limited so-called 'non-contact' time. These demands may be perceived as creating a 'tension' for HoDs, as they try to prioritize the tasks to be accomplished. On the one hand HoDs work alongside subject staff, engaging in reflective evaluation and playing a full part in the professional development of their colleagues, while on the other hand they also have to cope with the more traditional role of organizer and administrator. HoDs working in smaller schools seemed to be preoccupied with administration, mainly because there were few opportunities for delegation.

According to Bolam and Turner (1999), there appeared to be a wide variation in the amount of time set aside for HoDs to work in a more proactive fashion with departmental colleagues, with only eight out of twenty-three sample schools visited in their research allowing one hour or more each week, and four schools not allowing any extra time at all. A greater number of interruptions to classroom teaching occurred when the HoD carried some other whole-school responsibilities (e.g. site manager). Glover and Miller (1999b) noted that the demands on subject leaders (e.g. to sort out cover for absent colleagues, make sure resources are in the right place) were such as to overwhelm other equally pressing demands (e.g. monitoring and evaluation of teaching and learning).

Effective and ineffective subject departments

Sammons et al. (1997) found a number of factors which appeared to influence departmental performance, for example, high expectations

of the pupils by the staff, a strong academic emphasis, the existence of a shared vision, quality of teaching, HoDs' leadership and
teamwork.

Harris *et al.* (1997) investigated the 'key' features of effectively
managed departments. A small sample of schools was selected for
further study in the West of England. Value-added scores were
available for individual schools and individual subjects. The small
number of departments chosen (six, representing a range of subjects – English, Maths, Science and Humanities) were regarded as
being effective and had high value-added scores. Harris *et al.* (1997)
found evidence that the SMTs in each of the schools were trying to
build on good practice and raise the expectations of staff and pupils.
This might, for example, involve pupils in school decision-making
processes via the School Council. A great deal of emphasis was
placed on positive pupil behaviour and achievement. However,
some of the departmental staff did not feel they were operating in a
structure and culture which was supportive of their specialist endea-
vours. Nearly all the departmental staff interviewed believed that the
SMT was not sufficiently collegiate, in contrast with their own perceptions of greater democracy at departmental level. As a consequence, Harris *et al.* (1997) suggested that the management style of
the SMT appeared to be in stark contrast to the style of the successful
HoDs. As far as managing effective departments was concerned, the
results of the Harris *et al.* study showed that eleven features appeared
to be important in identifying departmental effectiveness, as can be
seen in Table 2.1.

Eight of these factors (denoted by an asterisk) could, in my
opinion, be considered as being directly attributable to the work of
subject leaders. Surprisingly, opportunities for training and professional development did not feature as a characteristic of an effective
department, which might have emerged if a larger sample of departments were researched.

Both the Sammons *et al.* (1997) and Harris *et al.* (1997) research
sought to identify the characteristics of effective subject departments
in secondary schools. Both studies shared some common features
regarding the characteristics of effective departments, but there
were some distinctive differences between the two investigations.
The most important of these differences concerned the Sammons
et al. finding that the whole-school context, in conjunction with the

Table 2.1 Key features of effective and ineffective departments

Features of effective departments	Features of ineffective departments
A collegiate management style*	Inappropriate leadership and management styles*
A strong vision of the subject translated at classroom level*	A lack of vision for the department and the subject*
Well organized in terms of assessment, record keeping and homework*	Poor organization*
Good resource management*	
Effective monitoring and evaluation*	Inadequate system for monitoring and evaluation*
Structured lessons and regular feedback	Poor communication within the department*
Clear routines and practices in classrooms	Non-collegial climate*
Syllabus (now referred to as a specification) matching the needs and abilities of pupils*	
Strong pupil-centred ethos that rewards pupils	
Opportunities for autonomous learning*	
Central focus on teaching and learning	Absence of professional development and learning*
	No leading professional within the department*

quality of leadership provided by the SMT, appeared to play a very significant role in enabling departments to function as effective units. If the support from the SMT was not forthcoming, expectations were low and the articulation of the goals of the school were not clear, then it was seen to be more difficult for departments to thrive. This was in contrast to the finding by Harris *et al.* (1997) that individual departments could operate very effectively almost in spite of the poor quality of leadership provided by the SMT.

The absence of high-quality leadership and its consequent potentially disastrous effects was revealed by the work of Harris (1998), who investigated the characteristics of *ineffective* departments in a total of eight departments covering a range of subjects in four different secondary schools in England. A set of *nine* common features was identified, of which *eight* could be directly attributed to the HoD (denoted by an asterisk, see Table 2.1).

It can be seen that most of these factors are simply the reverse of those features which are prevalent among effective departments (see Harris *et al.*, 1997). In addition Harris found a number of failure factors which could be associated with the quality of teaching (i.e. no team-teaching strategies employed and no opportunities for sharing good practice), teaching relationships (lack of teamwork and departmental staff working in relative isolation), and no emphasis on training to improve the standards of teaching. This suggests that the one central reason for departmental ineffectiveness is that the person responsible for the curriculum area is unable to provide the management and leadership skills which the departmental team needs. On the other hand, in order for a department to be effective, other factors need to be considered, apart from the team leader displaying the most appropriate forms of leadership and management in the context in which they work. These might include a commitment on the part of the departmental staff to deliver well-planned and clearly structured lessons and a willingness to adhere to agreed routines.

The appointment and subsequent work of both a highly effective Head of English (Myers, 1996) and a new Head of Science (OHMCI, 1996, p. 20) provide clear evidence of how to address the problems of an ineffective department.

A final body of relevant evidence gleaned from school inspections may be usefully included in this section. Ofsted (2002) note that there appear to be six key factors which are features of the most effective departments. The first and perhaps the most important aspect is the outstanding leadership provided by the SL, which can be inspirational for those working in the department. In this example, a clear vision for the teaching of English is outlined:

The vision of the Head of the English department centred on establishing an intellectual and aesthetic community in which literature, language, media, theatre and other performing arts were constantly discussed, practised and valued. This was associated with rich extra-curricular activities such as theatre visits, writing magazines, reading groups and drama or media productions. (p. 58)

A second feature was the opportunity for colleagues to observe each other teaching. Thirdly, the existence of a secure scheme of work which still allows scope for individual teacher creativity. A fourth important feature concerned the ways in which the subject teaching was geared to the needs of *all* the pupils. One example quoted illustrated the response of a History department to the challenge of stretching the more able pupils:

The History department was in the process of amending schemes of work to reflect a question-based approach that it had been developing for some time, and with a stronger emphasis on extended writing in order to move more pupils to the highest levels by the end of each key stage. The department also took the implications of diversity and inclusion very seriously, as well as the progress of more able pupils and the achievements of boys. (p. 63)

A fifth factor which characterized good departments was the consistent application of an assessment policy which explained clearly the procedures that all teachers should adopt to support the progress of the pupils. The following example indicates what pupils needed to do to improve the standards of their work in Key Stage 4:

In a science department . . . all Key Stage 4 pupils had been given a guide that set out what is required in science investigations in order to achieve each level. They also had writing frameworks to guide them through planning and preparation. Teachers structured their own oral and written feedback so that it related to pupils' progress towards targets and the specific action to improve. (p. 68)

The sixth factor which can enhance the performance of a department is the effective use of accommodation, resources and especially staff. Careful targeted support for non-subject specialists and learning-support assistants can greatly increase the standards of teaching and learning in any department.

Discussion points and practical activities
1. Reflect on the seven perspectives on leadership, described in the chapter. Assuming that subject leadership is about exerting influence over other colleagues, note down two examples, in Table 2.2 below, of where you feel that you have exercised this form of leadership during the last three months.

Table 2.2 Different perspectives on leadership

Type of leadership	Examples	Effectiveness
(a) Situational		
(b) Transformational		
(c) Moral		
(d) Political		
(e) Symbolic		
(f) Distributed		
(g) Team		

2. Rate your own effectiveness as a subject leader for each of the leadership perspectives in Table 2.2 using the following scale:

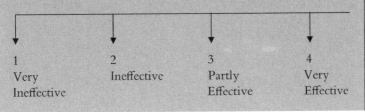

1	2	3	4
Very Ineffective	Ineffective	Partly Effective	Very Effective

3. Having completed Table 2.2, present your ideas for discussion with your line manager. As a result, suggest ways in which you might improve your effectiveness as a subject leader, for any of the leadership perspectives listed, as appropriate.
4. Examine the evidence for effective departments in Table 2.1. Where can improvements be made in your own department which might improve its effectiveness?
5. In your next discussion with your line manager, focus on the use of non-contact time. Reflect on the balance of time spent on purely administrative tasks and time allocated to improving teaching and learning in your subject.

Further reading

Bennis, W. and Nanus, B. (1985) *Leaders: The Strategies for Taking Charge*, New York: Harper Row.

Bolman, L. and Deal, T. (1991) *Reframing Organisations: Artistry, Choice and Leadership,* San Francisco: Jossey-Bass.

Harris, A. (2004) 'Distributed leadership and school improvement: leading or misleading?', *Educational Management, Administration and Leadership*, 32 (1): 11–24.

Helgesen, S. (1995) *The Female Advantage: Women's Ways of Leadership*, New York: Bantam Doubleday Dell.

Ruding, E. (2000) *Middle Management in Action: Practical Approaches to School Improvement*, London: RoutledgeFalmer.

Sergiovanni, T. J. (2001) *Leadership: What's in it for Schools?* London: RoutledgeFalmer.

3 Tasks to be done and strategies to be used

Introduction

The purpose of this chapter is to provide a bridge between the previous two chapters, which describe the working context of subject leaders and the next eight chapters, which discuss both the tasks to be carried out at departmental level and how they might be carried out, in the light of some recent research evidence.

At the outset, it is important to establish the nature of the responsibilities borne by all subject leaders in secondary schools in England and Wales. These include all aspects concerning the organization of resources in the department; monitoring classroom practice; managing the performance of departmental staff; ensuring that the curriculum is continually updated and providing training opportunities for all departmental staff. Promotion to the position of Head of Department (HoD) is usually achieved by an experienced member of staff with a proven track record of successful classroom teaching. Normally, he/she would be interviewed for such a post by the senior management in a school, in competition with other candidates. As the post carries the overall responsibility for the standards of teaching and learning in the department, HoDs generally receive extra salary increments in recognition of their additional managerial burden.

The TTA (1998) standards for subject leaders were introduced in Chapter 1. In this chapter, the four key task areas are fleshed out in more detail:

Strategic direction and development of the subject

This involves the subject leader drawing up departmental development plans on an annual basis in consultation with departmental staff; developing policies in line with those of the whole school in areas such as assessment and discipline and regularly monitoring the progress made towards agreed departmental targets. These issues are discussed in more detail in Chapter 7.

Teaching and learning

This is a collection of tasks designed to promote effective teaching and learning. It includes creating and updating schemes of work which meet the needs of pupils of all abilities (which is an extremely challenging responsibility for all subject leaders); ensuring that due attention is paid to the development of literacy, numeracy and ICT in the subject; using data to set appropriate targets for pupils; recording and reporting information on pupil progress; and providing opportunities for subject teachers to share good practice in departmental discussions.

Leading and managing staff

This is primarily concerned with the establishment and maintenance of good communication both within the department and among the wider school community. Other relevant aspects include being able to establish good working relationships among team members; working with the school's SENCO to ensure that individual education plans (IEPs) are drawn up and utilized to meet the needs of pupils; being able to work as a political leader in the best interests of the subject; being able to delegate responsibilities where appropriate and taking an active role in the professional development of staff, particularly in helping to meet some of the training needs of staff through the use of on-site INSET.

An explicit assumption which underpins these standards is that SLs take responsibility for their own professional development. Reference to this can be found in the self-management skills section of the TTA (1998) standards (p. 8).

Efficient and effective deployment of staff and resources

This aspect of the job involves drawing up departmental priorities in terms of curriculum development in line with whole-school action plans. The subject leader is responsible for managing a budget and for making bids to extend the range of subject teaching and learning activities when additional finance becomes available. It also involves giving advice to senior management about the most effective use of existing staff on the timetable. Some subject leaders need to consider how best to utilize support staff; for example, laboratory technicians in Science. A final aspect of this task entails attention being paid to safety issues as they apply in the subject being taught.

All of these task-based areas involve change to some degree. No improvement can occur without change. The policy initiatives outlined in Chapter 1 usually involve HoDs in the implementation of change. These ideas are discussed more in Chapter 6.

Most of the findings discussed in this chapter are based on the Phase 1 research, reported in detail in Turner (2002).

Tasks

The task of leading and managing a department is obviously going to depend first and foremost on its size. Regular formal and informal contact with only two or three other members of staff is usually far easier to achieve than in departments where there are as many as ten to twelve people teaching the subject. The ratio of full-time to part-time staff is an important factor as the SL needs to make a regular and conscious effort to maintain contact with part-time staff. Another consideration concerns the subject teaching commitments of full-time staff in other curriculum areas. It is often the case that departmental staff teach in different locations around the school, which is exacerbated if the school is split-site. It would be foolish to underestimate the potential advantages to an HoD of having a suite of rooms in the same location, to encourage regular formal and informal contact between staff and reduce the feeling of isolation, which can easily frustrate teachers. One final complicating factor is that subject leaders sometimes have to cope with staff who have significant whole-school responsibilities outside the department; for example, a member of the subject department might also be a member of the SMT.

Various aspects of the four key task areas will now be addressed in more detail.

Strategic direction and development of the subject

This will only occur if the SL has a clear vision of what good teaching and learning in the subject actually means. Equally, being able to share and build that vision among the departmental staff is a vital component. Being able to establish credibility among the departmental staff is an important priority for a newly appointed SL. Plans can then be drawn up for departmental development and raising standards of pupil achievement within a positive climate and a focus on learning. One corollary of this is that SLs become expert in the implementation of change, without which improvements will not occur. Depending on the nature of the change being proposed or introduced, it will usually require the HoD to work hard with his/her colleagues to accept and adopt the change. Occasionally, the SL will have to oppose a proposed change as the practical difficulties in its implementation may far outweigh any potential benefits.

In the current educational climate, all SLs have to be aware of their responsibilities as far as subject accountability is concerned. In that sense, being able to use data on pupil performance effectively as part of the monitoring of pupil progress is a skill which all SLs need to acquire. Similarly, being able to set targets for the subject in line with whole-school targets is an acquired skill as they need to contain an appropriate level of challenge and be achievable.

Managing teaching and learning

It is vital to set up schemes of work (SoWs) which involve the departmental staff in their construction. This encourages ownership of the curriculum without necessarily being over-prescriptive. A great deal of care is needed to construct SoWs which take account of the needs of all pupils, particularly those with learning difficulties and the small minority of very able or 'gifted' pupils. SLs can also advise on pedagogy, especially where more inexperienced staff are concerned. As part of the overall whole-school focus on improving literacy and numeracy skills, the SL can promote discussion and ask for ideas as to the best ways in which such skills can be developed. One important feature of an SL's work in this area would be monitoring standards of teaching and learning. One of the key features of an effectively managed department, according to the research of Harris et al. (1997), was the emphasis placed on recording pupils' progress and dealing with early signs of underachievement. Various forms of monitoring are possible, ranging from direct first-hand observation of classroom practice, gathering and collating module test data, checking a sample of exercise books from each member of the department to ensure that departmental policy guidelines are being followed, to brief, informal conversations with individual staff.

In the overall context of teaching and learning, a more recent performance-based task has gained prominence in the drive to raise standards. There is now a plethora of data readily available to members of the SMT which can be used to track the progress of individuals and groups from Year 7 onwards. Such data can also be used now to set departmental targets for KS3 SATs, for example, and pass rates at GCSE in terms of the percentage of pupils achieving five or more grades. The constant pressure to maintain and improve examination pass rates has led to certain groups of pupils, for example, those who are forecast to obtain a D grade at GCSE to receive more targeted help and advice from teachers. It is now quite common, for example, for schools to run GCSE revision classes for Year 11 in the Easter holidays with the sole aim of improving pass rates at GCSE.

Leading and managing the department

Inevitably, communication among staff in any department is an extremely important issue. Formally, this will tend to occur in departmental meetings, but these only take place infrequently. It is more likely that regular informal contacts between individuals or groups of staff will be of far greater significance. Most departments can usually establish a meeting place where social contacts can be facilitated and teachers can talk to each other about the practice of teaching. These contacts help to establish positive working relationships and add to a collegial climate.

Leading a department can also mean playing an important part in the professional development of departmental staff, especially inexperienced trainee teachers and those in the early years of their career. There has been very little attention paid as to how HoDs address the needs of their own departmental staff. According to Turner (2002), there were two major aspects to the part played by HoDs in the professional development of departmental staff. The first and most popular response focused on the work of the LEA as a provider of suitable, usually off-site INSET. The second most popular reply was the hands-on approach adopted by many HoDs in organizing on-site INSET, based mainly on the time available on the five annual training days during the school year. Hopkins and Harris (2000) argued that the use of both of these strategies demonstrates a commitment to staff development and they may be complementary in their objectives.

Effective deployment of staff and resources

This area of an SL's work includes drawing up priorities for expenditure on departmental resources, using accommodation in a stimulating manner and regularly assessing standards of safety in the teaching of the subject. To what extent subject leaders influence the decisions about sharing out the teaching load among departmental colleagues is a matter of continuing debate.

Strategies
There are numerous ways in which HoDs can actually work with departmental staff either individually or as a group as well as parents and pupils which will help them to fulfil their responsibilities.

Working with individuals
Many activities, (for example, team teaching with departmental colleagues; INSET; classroom observation of colleagues; encouraging departmental staff to observe each other teach), are only used occasionally by HoDs. SLs running on-site INSET is a regular feature of the five annual non-teaching days and does occur occasionally at other times during the school year. Bolam and Turner (1999) found that SLs regarded on-site INSET very favourably, particularly in relation to curriculum development and the sharing of good practice, but, not surprisingly, were less enthusiastic about the value of off-site in-service training. Field et al. (2000) commented rather negatively on the value of off-site INSET when they noted that:

> the updating of subject knowledge and indeed all forms of professional competence has in some ways been hindered by the trend towards a 'consultancy model' of in-service training which involves the cascading of training outcomes by one teacher to others within a team. (p. 174)

The one exception to this trend can be seen in the views of Heads of Technology who were more positive in their perceptions of the usefulness of local consortia organizing training for small groups of staff. I found that HoDs were almost equally divided concerning the value of off-site INSET (Turner, 2000). Those who held more negative views focused mainly on the fact that the courses on offer did not really appear to address the needs of departmental staff. Very often the most that might be expected of those attending such courses was that their awareness had been raised of particular issues (for example, receiving information about the latest computer software). On the other hand, almost three-quarters of those interviewed did feel that on-site INSET generally met the needs of the staff and tended to be more focused on teaching and learning issues. Field *et al.* (2000) advocated SLs exploiting the potential which peer coaching (Joyce and Showers, 1988) and micro-teaching (Wallace, 1991) have in sharing new ideas with departmental colleagues. However, Field *et al.* (2000) felt that on-site INSET does run the risk that it can lead to a 'recycling of existing, even stale ideas' (p. 174).

Coaching has been advocated by various commentators, for example Tomlinson (1998), as a way of improving departmental performance. He argued that the main purpose of coaching was: to 'improve teaching and learning, by encouraging teachers to work together as colleagues' (p. 37). He felt that this process can take different forms: peer supervision; collegial supervision; peer review; team coaching; mentoring; observation; and cognitive coaching. However, this process is only likely to be effective with very inexperienced or trainee teachers. Some experienced 'dyed-in-the-wool' staff may respond rather negatively to the idea of being coached by one of their colleagues. However, part of the job of being a subject leader entails taking risks in order to bring about desired change.

One exception to this scenario could be when the department is considering how best to incorporate greater use of ICT in subject teaching. Often newly qualified teachers (NQTs) or trainee teachers have a much more positive attitude and more comprehensive set of skills which could well lead them to be asked by the subject leader to demonstrate new software or hardware to the rest of the department during an INSET session. This does not guarantee changes in classroom behaviour but can be an important first step in overcoming resistance among colleagues.

Classroom observation may now be used more frequently by SLs, following the introduction of performance management. Bolam and Turner (1999) found that:

> the views about the monitoring of staff work were mixed. Whilst many of the HoDs interviewed expressed their frustration at having very little time to observe members of the department teaching, a few did mention classroom observation of their colleagues as a high priority, if an individual had identified weaknesses. (p. 252)

However, there was more enthusiasm for SLs to engage in this process, as a means of monitoring the progress of very inexperienced teachers and contributing towards their professional development. Estyn (1999) found evidence that departments were reviewed by the SMT on a bi-annual basis. However, the best well-managed departments engaged in departmental self-review on a regular basis.

My research indicated that HoDs felt that they used departmental meetings in three ways, which may be perceived as being influential in improving teaching and learning (Turner, 2002). Firstly they can be used to discuss issues relating to curriculum development; secondly, they provide opportunities for sharing good practice and thirdly, to build up team spirit. Discussion based around the provision for SEN pupils or the bidding for more resources may not be as influential. The reasons for this may in part be due to a desire on the part of HoDs to encourage members of the department to work together to solve problems which occur in everyday classroom practice, leaving other aspects such as special needs provision to be decided by the HoD him/herself without recourse to a great deal of consultation.

Working with staff in departmental meetings

Although the frequency of departmental meetings varies from school to school, they do occur regularly on a formal and informal basis. They provide opportunities to deal with important managerial issues (e.g. organizing human and material resources) as well as providing the HoD with the opportunity to build and share a vision for the teaching of the subject. According to Field *et al.* (2000):

chairing meetings requires meticulous preparation and planning, an atmosphere that is conducive to free and open discussion and well developed inter-personal skills. (p. 231)

Using departmental meetings to plan the curriculum and share good practice are commonly used strategies. This echoes Hammond's (1998) ideas, who noted that professional craft knowledge needed to be shared among departmental colleagues. He commented that:

department meetings, schemes of work and the teacher's workroom all have their role in turning *good practice* into *common practice*. (p. 30)

However, it was clear the HoDs used departmental meetings for other purposes, such as promoting team spirit, because they recognize the importance of high morale and motivational levels.

Torrington and Weightman (1990) suggested that HoDs try to create within their departments a culture of shared basic assumptions and values together with the potentially beneficial aspects of collaborative teamwork. According to Busher and Harris (2000), subject leaders have the major responsibility for the creation of social cohesion within the department. This is no easy task, particularly in large departments which may contain some staff who may work in the department part-time or who work in other departments. They warn that if the cultures SLs construct are dysfunctional:

people in the subject area will not be helped to meet its purposes or those of the school. Staff in such cultures may be isolated from each other, not working as effective teams. (p. 6)

In departmental meetings, HoDs can attempt to achieve a consensus of opinion on a particular issue. They provide a potentially useful forum for discussion of issues which need to be clarified and the promotion of a collegial climate of participative decision-making. Bennett (1999) noted that the TTA standards for subject leaders appeared to create confusion in the area of decision-making because, on the one hand they assume line-manager accountability, and on the other hand strongly advocate that SLs generate a climate of collegiality with an emphasis on teamwork. However, this is partly a reflection of the complex and ambiguous nature of subject leadership where post-holders are expected to fulfil a liaison role, i.e. as both an arbitrator of whole-school policy while at the same time representing the views of the departmental staff to the SMT.

Brown et al.'s (2000) work indicated wide variations of practice in regard to participation in whole-school decision-making. They concluded that middle managers wanted:

a greater say in decisions about the school. . . . SLs want bureaucratic approaches to leadership to be replaced by distributed leadership throughout the school. (pp. 328–9).

Such collegial practice is not without its critics. Collegiality can take various forms, each of which has different consequences. Hargreaves (1992) mounted quite a sharp criticism of collegiality, calling it 'contrived', on the basis of his own research in elementary (primary) schools in Canada. He felt that the decision-making process was contrived in the sense that a decision on a particular issue had already been made in advance (usually by the SMT) and the consultation process with staff was really no more than either a paper exercise or 'going through the motions'. The same could be said for some forms of decision-making in secondary schools.

Monitoring pupils' work is a commonly used strategy by most SLs. The results of such an exercise can form the basis of a most productive departmental discussion in a meeting of staff. Field et al. (2000) pointed out that there are two essential prerequisites for this process:

Firstly, the subject leader and team member must share a collective understanding of what learning is in relation to the particular subject. A second key factor should be that class teachers are responsible for monitoring themselves. (p. 190)

The ways in which the monitoring process occurred can be quite varied. Some SLs place more emphasis on the use of a formal procedure, examining samples of pupils' work on a regular basis. Heads of English spend a great deal of time on moderation of coursework, to ensure internal consistency. The importance of monitoring was stressed by Hammond (1998) when he noted that monitoring procedures need to be in place if departments are to avoid what he referred to as a 'natural tendency to be entropic'.

Working with parents and pupils

In my own research subject leaders' contacts with parents were spasmodic and therefore it was no surprise that activities such as interviewing parents, inviting parents in to see pupils at work, or using parents' evenings to show them examples of pupils' work, were only used occasionally (see Turner, 2002 for more details). However, two features of their work with pupils were mentioned as being used more frequently; namely, monitoring pupils' work and the display of pupils' work. HoDs justified their support for the display of pupils' work, especially in English and Technology, because they felt that it indicated to other pupils the standard of quality products required to achieve high marks. The display of pupils' work has the additional benefit of enabling pupils and teachers to feel that their efforts are valued and appreciated by a wider community. One HoD felt that it was part of her job to:

> notice things, to notice displays that have been put up; to notice techniques that are being experimented with; to notice the work children produce in a particular class and to praise it and reinforce it. (Bolam and Turner, 1999, p. 254)

Summary

Table 3.1 tries to summarize the relationship between the tasks to be done and the methods or strategies which might be used when tackling these jobs.

Bolam and Turner (1999) found that many of the HoDs they interviewed felt that:

> it was the combination of methods which they used (i.e. a holistic approach) rather than one particular method, which was the most instrumental in dealing with problems and improving teaching within the department. (p. 256)

This indicates that over-reliance on one particular strategy or method may not be very effective in terms of subject leadership.

Table 3.1   The relationship between the tasks for which HoDs have direct responsibility and the methods by which they may be tackled

Tasks to be addressed by SLs	Examples of methods or strategies to be used by SLs
A The Strategic Direction and Development of the Subject: 'Within the context of the school's aims and policies, subject leaders develop and implement subject policies, plans, targets and practices' (p. 10)	Meetings to discuss: • departmental policy – for example in relation to discipline, assessment, homework and equal opportunities • sharing good practice in a collegial climate where all colleagues can actively participate in decision-making • inspection evidence, examination results and current education policies to plan changes to the curriculum To work with individual staff to evaluate the quality of their own teaching
B Teaching and Learning: 'Subject leaders secure and sustain effective teaching of the subject, evaluate the quality of teaching and standards of pupils' achievements and targets for improvement' (p. 10)	The HoD occasionally observes classroom teaching (informally) and more formally within the performance management cycle in order to influence the quality of teaching and learning The HoD holds meetings to discuss pedagogical issues concerning teaching and learning Monitoring the quality of pupils' work frequently
C Leading and Managing Staff: 'Subject leaders provide to all those with involvement in the teaching or support of the subject, the support, challenge, information and development necessary to sustain motivation and secure improvement in teaching' (p.11)	The HoD leads INSET sessions and coaches individuals where appropriate The HoD uses meetings to discuss: • the arrangements for the teaching of SEN pupils • the introduction of curriculum innovations HoD leads by example concerning the display of pupils' work Where appropriate, the HoD works with a member of staff in a team-teaching situation

Table 3.1   *(continued)*

Tasks to be addressed by SLs	Examples of methods or strategies to be used by SLs
D The Effective Deployment of Staff and Resources: 'Subject leaders identify appropriate resources for the subject and ensure they are used efficiently, effectively and safely' (p. 12)	The HoD organizes the matching of staff to appropriate classes, where this is possible. The HoD may also use departmental meetings to discuss the use of resources and safety issues

The nature of departmental work usually depends on collaboration and frequent contact between departmental staff. Such contacts are informal and sometimes unplanned. This is reflected in the comments made by Bolam and Turner (1999) who noted that:

> HoDs valued and deliberately engineered regular informal contacts. 'Popping in and out' of classrooms, spending time with staff at break times and lunch times, socialising out of school, were all seen as useful mechanisms for acquiring and communicating information. (p. 252)

Discussion points
1. What criteria should a subject leader use when deciding how best to deploy his/her colleagues when allocating staff to teaching groups?
2. To what extent would you say decision-making in your subject department is 'contrived' as Hargreaves (1992) suggests?
3. Scrutinize Table 3.1 carefully. What other methods or strategies might be used by a subject leader to meet the requirements of each of the four task areas described?
4. As an existing HoD:
   (a) to what extent are you able to delegate tasks to other members of the departmental team?
   (b) summarize the main problems which can arise when delegating tasks and suggest ways in which they might be minimized

5. To what extent do you agree/disagree that departmental meetings should have the following features:
   (a) a clearly stated finish time
   (b) no meeting lasting more than one hour
   (c) a written agenda, circulated to all participiants beforehand
   (d) give all participants at the meeting the chance to express their opinions on contentious issues
   For further information, see Field *et al.* (2000), p. 222–33.

Further reading

Busher, H. and Saran, R. (1995) *Managing Teachers as Professionals in Schools*, London: Kogan Page.

Everard, K. B., Morris, G. and Wilson, I. (2004) *Effective School Management*, London: Paul Chapman.

Gold, A. (1998) Head *of Department: Principles in Practice*, London: Cassell.

Ofsted (1997) *Subject Management in Secondary Schools: Aspects of Good Practice*, London: Ofsted.

Ruding, E. (2000) *Middle Management in Action: Practical Approaches to School Improvement*, London: RoutledgeFalmer

Turner, C. K. (2003) 'A critical review of research on subject leaders in secondary schools', *School Leadership and Management* 23 (2): 209–27.

4 The subject leader as team leader

Introduction

The main aim of this chapter is to discuss two main themes:

(i) the notion of teamwork in a departmental context, and
(ii) the subject leader as a team leader and some of the problems which are associated with working in this way

In order to fulfil the responsibilities and expectations of subject leaders, one of the best strategies which can be employed involves the use of teamwork based around subject departments. The establishment of a climate of collegiality among the departmental staff has become a high priority for subject leaders, involving departmental staff participating in decision-making in both informal settings (socializing during lunch times) and more formally in department meetings.

Teams in secondary schools vary considerably especially at a subject level. These variations are characterized by differences between the sizes of teams, the frequency with which team members meet, the age and experience of team members, the gender balance in the team, the credibility of the team leader in the 'eyes' of the team members and, above all else, the loyalty of the team members to the team itself. If a team leader has one or more members of the SMT in his/her department, these divided loyalties can be very difficult to handle. For example, the attendance at team meetings by a member of the school's SMT can be spasmodic, making it difficult to ensure they are fully briefed about current developments concerning teaching and learning within the subject.

In the final section of this chapter, some case-study evidence is presented of a successful Head of English describing her views about team leadership while working in a secondary school in Wales.

Effective teams and teamwork

Terrell and Terrell (in Brundrett and Terrell, 2004, p. 126) argue for the existence of fifteen characteristics of an effective team. However, they each have implications for the ways in which each team leader works, and I have tried to explain what they might be (see Table 4.1 below).

Underpinning much of the team leader's work is the notion of collegiality. According to Bennett (2003), 'there is a very strong rhetoric of collegiality in how middle leaders describe the culture of their departments' (p. 1). Bush (2003) argued that collegial models of management in education include the following features: an authority based on subject expertise; a common set of values held by members of the team; participation by all team members in decision-making; and that decisions themselves are reached by consensus. However, interpreting teamwork in a collegial sense does not necessarily offer subject leaders a panacea. Problems may arise if certain team members appear to agree with a collegial approach to decision-making and their behaviour in a meeting may indicate that they have assented to the decisions made in for example, a departmental meeting. However, their subsequent behaviour shows that, far from following the agreed procedure, they attempt to subvert the process to fit in with their own position/perception of the solution to the questions raised.

According to Field *et al.* (2000), it is worth team leaders spending time reflecting on the following five key components if they are seeking to improve teamwork in the department. (I have added my own comments alongside each bullet point.)

- *Purposes and objectives of the team*: this might involve regularly reviewing schemes of work and updating them as necessary; the use of various forms of assessment by subject teachers; reviewing departmental plans in the light of whole-school initiatives

Table 4.1   The characteristics of an effective team and their implications for subject leaders

Team characteristic	Implications for team leaders and their work
Shared goals	If the team leader can build a 'vision' of what the department is aiming to achieve by discussion and consensus building, then he/she can generate a situation where the team members 'buy in' to the departmental plans and feel a sense of ownership.
Focus on what matters	The central focus should be on teaching and learning. Formal and informal meetings do give opportunities for sharing good practice within the team.
Sense of team identity	This is largely built collectively but the team leader does have the primary responsibility to encourage a sense of belonging. There needs to be plenty of opportunity for social interactions between group members to occur.
Good communication	This becomes very important if team members work in different areas in the school or the school itself is split-site.
Trust	Delegation of responsibilities gives the team leader the chance to give individual team members delegated responsibilities and build mutual trust.
Willingness to work through and utilize professional differences	From time to time, departmental staff will express a variety of opinions about the best ways to implement policies; for example, in connection with behaviour management or in the use of ICT in their lessons. The skill of the team leader lies as much in being able to tolerate these differences as in ensuring that all members of the team are working towards the same agreed goals.

Table 4.1   *(continued)*

Team characteristic	Implications for team leaders and their work
High expectations	Again, this notion cannot be followed through if the team leader does not have high expectations of themselves. They can be communicated to parents and pupils in a variety of ways.
Clear procedures and ground rules	Departmental sub-culture is established on the basis of consent and discussion. The team leader needs to think carefully about reviewing the effectiveness of the policies being implemented on a regular basis.
Team members whose skills and experience are complementary	Team leaders have limited influence over the composition of their team at the departmental level. Therefore, one of the main tasks here is try to improve the portfolio of skills and experience within the subject by encouraging individuals to attend INSET courses which address specific needs.
Opportunities and encouragement for every one to contribute	This is achieved on a one-to-one basis and in group discussion in departmental meetings. It is no easy task to ensure that each member of the team feels valued but often a straightforward expression of thanks can acknowledge the work of others and engender a feeling of being appreciated. This element also assumes that the subject leader is willing to listen to the suggestions of other departmental staff.
An ability to find and use information to make decisions	It is assumed here that the information collected would be relevant. However, it is worth noting that team leaders can sometimes propose perfectly rational solutions to problems which later turn out to be flawed.

Table 4.1   (*continued*)

Team characteristic	Implications for team leaders and their work
Flexibility to work in a variety of ways and share leadership	Notions of distributed leadership equally apply at the departmental level. All team leaders will have their own combination of strengths and weaknesses. The existence of a well-balanced team means that a team leader can devolve responsibility for leading the team forward in specific circumstances. For example, even a trainee teacher can lead an INSET session on the use of ICT software if it is deemed to be appropriate.
Encourage the individual development of team members	This is also reliant on the team leader being able to encourage departmental staff to attend appropriate INSET courses and being willing to organize and deliver school-based training.
Seek appropriate external support and resources	Here the team leader is acting more as a political leader in the sense that, to achieve such support, can require a great deal of bargaining and negotiation with the SMT in a liaison role.
Willingness to evaluate the effectiveness of the team	This can partly depend of the stability of team. If one or more members of the team are absent for lengthy periods of time, the team leader may find all their energy being devoted to surviving on a day-by-day basis.

- *How the team will work*: this would involve clarifying how frequently the team would meet; how decisions made will be communicated through minutes of meetings
- *How the objectives will be achieved*: this really involves discussing who is going to do what and by when. It is therefore normally a delegation of responsibilities in order to achieve these objectives which would not be possible by one person. That

said, in one-person subject departments, it is that individual who may wish to reflect upon current practice with their line manager when teamwork would otherwise be impossible

- *How resources will be deployed*: this aspect incorporates both the deployment and use of material resources as well as human beings. Knowing the strengths and weaknesses of each team member is vital to successful deployment
- *How the performance of the team will be reviewed and monitored*: performance data in the form of KS3 tests and end-of-module tests are useful in guiding discussions about future improvements. Asking each team member to write down where they feel their teaching has gone well and where it might be improved can also help the team leader monitor progress. Pupils can also be asked similar questions in terms of identifying where they are finding problems with the work in the subject (p. 239–40)

Gold (1998) has discussed team development in terms of four stages of growth, including a consideration of the dynamics of a newly formed team (*forming*), characterized by confusion, anxiety and a 'wait and see how things turn out' attitude; *storming* when conflicts and subgroups can emerge; *norming* when mutual support develops and differences are put aside; and *performing* when a team matures and there is openness, flexibility, risk-taking and a high level of trust among team members. It should be noted that it is rare for a subject leader to work with a newly formed team at the time of his/her appointment. Generally most of the departmental staff are already in post and therefore the subject leader would need to exercise caution and assess the extent to which the team was operating effectively before introducing any significant changes to the ways in which the team functions.

Departmental staff spending time together off timetable or as part of a training day focusing on a specific issue can enable the team leader to promote greater teamwork and cohesion.

Teamwork in meetings

Teachers spend much of their time in school working in classrooms with pupils and classroom assistants. It is only when the departmental staff meet as a group at, say, lunchtimes that specific issues relating to teaching and learning may be addressed in formal meetings. Busher and Harris (2000) argued that when team leaders are seeking to chair their departmental meetings effectively, they need to bear in mind the need to:

- Allow space for colleagues to contribute to the discussion
- Bring colleagues into the discussion or sometimes to exclude them
- Take the lead in shaping ideas in the discussion when appropriate
- Paraphrase and sum up the discussion as the meeting progresses
- Draw together the threads of a discussion at its conclusion
- Help colleagues devise realistic steps for action (p. 117–18)

Limitations of teamwork

O'Neill (1997) sounds a note of caution about teamwork by arguing that teaching is still an activity where an individual may be isolated from his/her colleagues for much of the working day. An over-emphasis on teamwork may lead some teachers to feel a loss of control of their professional work by needing to conform to the 'group' decision to adopt certain teaching methods when individuals harbour some reservations about the use of such methods. Fullan (1999) argues against 'groupthink' which he defines as what happens when: 'people in a tightly knit culture go along uncritically with the group and/or squelch individual dissent' (p. 16). Wallace and Hall (1994) argued that there are problems with team approaches in the management of a school, whose structures have been traditionally hierarchical, if it is intended that each member of a team has a part to play in the decision-making process. Accordingly, they believe that teamwork is most effectively used when there is what they refer to as 'shared uncertainty' in the problem-solving process and no simple solution is immediately obvious. At the heart of this issue lies a paradox. Within the hierarchical structure of any secondary school, subject leaders are paid to take on extra responsibilities and sometimes make difficult decisions for the long term 'good' of the school. At the same time, the subject leader might encourage the use of teamwork to solve problems in departmental meetings, producing a solution, which is unacceptable to the SMT and then have to be realistic enough to admit that the use of such an approach may lead to a loss of morale among the staff.

Being a team leader

The TTA (1998) standards indicate that subject leaders should: 'establish clear expectations and constructive working relationships among staff involved with the subject' (p. 1). In addition, there are team leadership skills which are described in the TTA document. For example, subject leaders should be able to: 'secure commitment to a clear aim and direction for the subject and be able to work as part of team themselves' (p. 7). They should be able to deal sensitively with people, recognize individual needs and take account of them in securing a consistent team approach to raising achievement.

Whittaker (1993, p. 76) cites the work of Adair (1987) who identified five features of leadership, which are all relevant to the notion of subject leaders as team leaders:

Direction	Leaders are concerned to find new ways forward, to generate a clear sense of movement and direction.
Inspiration	Leaders have ideas and thoughts that are strong motivators for the working team, creating a directional energy.
Building teams	Leaders see teams as the natural and most effective form of management and spend their time in encouraging and coaching.
Example	It is not only what leaders do that affects others in the organization but how they do it.
Acceptance	Managers can be designated by title but do not become leaders until that appointment becomes ratified in the hearts and minds of the followers.

'New ways forward' usually concern curriculum development, pedagogical innovation, or the subject leader suggesting new forms of assessment. Motivating others may be dependent on the amount of experience other departmental staff have had.

Building teams means developing a sense of coherence and unity of purpose. It may not involve much in the way of direct coaching, because subject leaders generally have heavy teaching loads and are liable to concentrate their efforts on trainee teachers or newly qualified staff. Leading by example is more implicit than departmental staff often realize but it certainly does involve the subject leader setting and maintaining high standards for themselves.

Acceptance is bound up with notions of credibility, as a precursor to the subject leader being able to operate as a transformational team leader. The credibility of a subject leader is established among his/her colleagues based on being able to demonstrate high standards of teaching and learning and gaining their respect.

Problems faced by team leaders

Team leaders face a number of difficulties when trying to promote teamwork. Individual staff can often belong to a number of different teams that can compete for time together during the five annual training days. If one of the team members is part of the SMT, then sometimes they can be unavailable to participate in team activities. Sammons et al. (1997) identified a number of factors which inhibited teamwork, including personality conflicts between members of the department; staff absence; staff shortages; low morale and high staff turnover. They were all perceived to be possible barriers to team development.

Wise and Busher (2001) argue that if a subject leader does not establish good working relationships with the SMT, then he/she cannot represent the department effectively. Similarly, if the subject leader fails to build and sustain a collegial culture in the department, then standards of teaching and learning may well fall if members of the team feel isolated and unsupported. The consequences of a lack of collegiality can be far-reaching. Evidence from Harris's (1998) research into ineffective departments shows that there was little or no informal communication between team members and departmental meetings (so important for generating a sense of team identity and providing a forum for discussion of ideas and sharing good practice) were rarely held and poorly attended. This lack of collegiality meant that team members had little idea how other staff taught and there was little scope for discussion around trying out new teaching techniques to improve the quality of pupil learning.

There may be resistance among the departmental staff to greater emphasis being placed on teamwork by the subject leader. Katzenbach and Smith (1993) suggested there are three sources of resistance to teamwork:

- a lack of conviction about the need for teamwork, based partly on the fact that teaching a class is usually an isolated activity
- personal discomfort and the risk involved in working closely with others
- weak organizational performance ethics, where the SMT or subject leaders (or both) do not place much emphasis on achieving high standards

Some teachers value their autonomy and prefer to work on their own, feeling a sense of responsibility for their own teaching groups and find it difficult to work with other staff whom they do not rate very highly. As a consequence individual staff may feel that time spent in frequent meetings might be better spent in other ways. I think that teamwork is highly rated by all HoDs but its importance should never be underestimated. Getting all departmental staff to play their part in the team can be a time-consuming business requiring patience and persistence on the part of the subject leader.

Case study evidence

Research methodology
This section provides some evidence from a case study as a way of illustrating the key issues concerning team leadership. It discusses the views of a subject leader and two members of the departmental team, who were interviewed as part of Phase 2 of the research. The names used are not their real names to protect confidentiality. It focuses on one Head of English (Jackie), relatively newly appointed, having only been in post for two terms. She had already been teaching for 17 years at the time of the interview and had been a subject leader in her previous school. She was acknowledged by her Headteacher as being a very experienced and effective practitioner.

It was anticipated that the two departmental staff interviewed would be conscious of changes that had been recently introduced.

The person holding the responsibility for being 'second in the English department' (Sue) had acquired 12 years' teaching experience. She had been teaching in the school just over two years. The other member of the English department interviewed (Alison) had been in teaching for five years, having been working for three years in her present job.

The same questions (phrased appropriately) were posed to the Head of English and two members of her department. This gave the opportunity for some degree of triangulation to take place in the analysis of the following comments. The ideas about team leadership came from questions about acting as a departmental team leader. The responses deal with the team leader being a role model; securing a vision for the teaching of the subject; working with the SMT; willingness to accept the suggestions of others; and expressing appreciation for the efforts of team members.

Findings

Jackie felt that she was strongly encouraging the team approach within the department. She was deliberately grouping younger, less experienced staff with more experienced teachers in revising modules in the schemes of work in Key Stage 3.

Being a role model

> I do believe the head of department is a role model and that's why I think the most important thing that the head of department can do is to put time into teaching. The head of department has to be a good teacher, preferably, although this doesn't happen every week. They've got to be the best teacher in the department, because unless you are always updating and changing and modifying your own teaching, you can't expect anyone else to.

She is obviously very aware of the need to establish her own credibility with her colleagues, as well as leading by example. Sue also recognizes the need to be a role model; although, because she is already well established as a teacher, her perception is different from that of Alison, the younger member of staff – she is more cautious in her response.

Yes, except in the sense that it's always a problem for teachers because the actual practice of our craft if you like, is done in privacy. So that support teachers for instance will have quite a wide experience of observing other people teach but if you are predominantly a classroom teacher yourself you very rarely get the chance to see others perform. (Sue)

Alison alluded to some of the problems faced by any subject leader who wants to challenge the status quo. It represents one of the biggest problems for subject leaders: how to move the department forward without causing unnecessary splits and divisions between departmental staff.

Definitely a role model for other members for the departmental staff. That's been something here that my head of department has had to deal with because I think she came into a very traditional, old-fashioned department. Some people had been here quite a long time and to try and change things I think has been very difficult for her. I think she found it very hard to avoid the split of the teachers who wanted to move forward and do things in a different way and people who were sort of happy with the way things were. (Alison)

Being able to secure a vision for the teaching of the subject

Sharing of vision is important but having the vision in the first place is even more important because that's one of the things that I have noted about heads of department very often is that they don't have a vision about teaching or anything else much. (Jackie)

Jackie, as Head of English, is clear about the importance of creating and sharing a vision for the teaching of the subject. Both members of the departmental team indicate that she has been successful in communicating the nature of that vision within the department.

I certainly think my head of department has a very clear vision herself of what English means to her and what the teaching of English is and can be. Certainly she's excellent at conveying her

own enthusiasm and passion for that within departmental meetings and within less structured situations, and I think that is to a
very large extent contagious because if her enthusiasm is very real
then inevitably some of it rubs off onto the rest of the department
and encourages and fosters the enthusiasm and the commitment
that we feel on our own. (Sue)

Working with the senior management team (SMT)
The following comments indicate the difficulties that a subject leader
can experience in fulfilling their liaison role:

> Working with the senior management team on behalf of the
> department I've always found one of the most problematic areas
> of being a head of department, for the simple reason of how do
> you do it. Obviously you speak up for your department in
> whichever forum you're in but senior management teams every-
> where, it seems to me, are very elusive and hard to pin down and
> difficult to deal with and not really interested in the nitty gritty of
> department business, otherwise they'd still be heads of depart-
> ment. (Jackie)

Her efforts in representing the views of the departmental team are
appreciated by Sue, the second-in-department:

> She feels very passionately about her department and therefore
> represents it with commitment to the senior management team
> and will fight its corner which is reassuring for the rest of us.

Being open to the suggestions of others
Jackie indicates the almost subversive manner in which subject
leaders have to operate. Knowing what is required is an essential prerequisite but how a subject leader achieves the desired outcome is
something else!

> I think that a subtle head of department plants the seeds of sugges-
> tions that she's going to get. I always like to make people feel that
> it's their idea even if it's mine. The way to do that is to plant that
> seed in them before a meeting or pick up a point that they've
> made so that when you get to the meeting, you can say 'I think

you've got something to say on this' and then it's not always coming from you. That sounds very Machiavellian, but I think that you have to be a good manager of people if you're going to get the things that you want. (Jackie)

The following comments made by Sue confirm the subtle way in which suggestions from others are being picked up, but she goes on to note that they have to be in line with what the subject leader wants, in order to be taken up.

Suggestions – yes – but because of her clear vision, they do need to coincide perhaps with hers in order to progress. She certainly expresses appreciation for the efforts and commitment shown by the department no problem about that at all. (Sue)

Expressing appreciation for the efforts of others
Jackie, as team leader, recognizes the importance of making sure that the efforts of other departmental staff are valued and encouraged:

I think individuals need to feel valued and I think it is the subject leader's job to show them that they are.

This is confirmed by Alison who acknowledges the subject leader's expertise in this area.

She is very, very good at praising, because I think that is a real skill – I think I'd find it quite difficult, but she is very, very good at praising you and expresses appreciation for the efforts made.

Lessons to be learned about teamwork

In many ways, the quality of the teamwork currently in operation in the department is something which the subject leader is constantly trying to improve. To build an effective team requires time, patience and hard graft as well as a baseline of an appropriate amount of experience working with other professionals. Clearly, for a team leader to be successful, they need to be a good role model especially in the 'eyes' of the younger, less experienced staff. Whether the team leader needs to be the best teacher in the department is more contentious. It may be more important for them to be, first and foremost, a good role model. They also need to have developed their own clear vision for teaching and learning in the subject. This is usually the result of exposure to ideas in different school settings where the subject leader has worked under other Heads of Department. It requires a degree of self-confidence to work with members of the SMT in a liaison role. Here the subject leader is representing the views of the departmental staff to senior managers. Being willing to take 'on board' other peoples' suggestions also requires the team leader to be flexible in their approach. This can then lead to the team leader being willing to let go of the reins of power so that others can lead in ways which benefit the whole department. To be able to express appreciation and thanks for what staff are doing or have done without embarrassing them in any way is a vital skill for any team leader to acquire.

Even so, not all staff view teamwork in the same positive light. The encouragement for all to participate in decision-making is fine as long as there is no team member who is disillusioned or uncooperative. Perhaps an evaluation of the team's performance can be carried out on an annual basis when departmental plans are reviewed.

The multiplicity of teams in existence in any given school can mean that team members' loyalties are divided, particularly if one or more are members of the SMT. In addition if there are any part-time staff working in the department, then it can be difficult for the subject leader to ensure that they feel valued and are participating fully in the life of the department.

Discussion points and practical activities

1. What would you say are the characteristics of a subject leader who is a good team leader? Refer back to the ideas of Whittaker (1993) described in this chapter.

2. Table 4.2 below includes 15 characteristics of an effective team. Using the following four-point scale, complete Table 4.2 for your own department.

1	2	3	4
Very Good	Good	Satisfactory	Poor

Table 4.2   Characteristics of an effective team

Team characteristic	My rating	Average departmental rating
Shared goals		
Focus on what matters		
Sense of team identity		
Good communication		
Trust		
Willingness to accept the views of others		
High expectations		
Clear procedures		
Complementary skills and experience in the team		
Encouragement to contribute		
Can find information to use in decision-making		
Encouragement of individuals		
Flexibility in work		
Seek external support and resources		
Be willing to evaluate the team effectiveness		

3. Ask all the departmental team to give their views of the team's effectiveness anonymously and calculate the departmental average.
4. Where there are discrepancies between your views and those of the departmental team, discuss possible strategies for improving the team's effectiveness in your next departmental meeting.

Further reading

Belbin, R. M. (1993) *Management Teams: Why They Succeed or Fail*, Oxford: Butterworth-Heinemann.

Bell, L. (1992) *Managing Teams in Secondary Schools*, London: Routledge.

Bell, L. (1997) 'Staff teams and their management' in Crawford, M., Kydd, L. and Riches, C. *Leadership and Teams in Educational Management*, Buckingham: Open University Press.

Gold, A. (1998) *Head of Department: Principles in Practice*, London: Cassell.

Kydd, L., Anderson, L. and Newton, W. (2003) *Leading People and Teams in Education*, London: Paul Chapman.

5 Managing departmental relationships: a conflict perspective

Introduction

As can be seen in Chapter 4, there is a great deal to be gained by departments in secondary schools engaging in teamwork in a climate of collegiality (Field *et al.*, 2000). When dealing with departmental staff, the preferred model of operation is for the subject leader to act as a transformational leader, according to Busher and Harris (2000), who can focus on: 'building trust and shared values (collegiality) between staff in a school' (p. 111).

According to the TTA (1998) standards for subject leaders, SLs are expected to: 'establish constructive working relationships among staff, involved with the subject, including through team working and mutual support' (p. 11) and: 'ensure that the headteacher, senior managers and governors are well informed about subject policies, plans and priorities' (p. 12).

All of this is presented in an unproblematic manner. It ignores the micropolitical context in which SLs have to work, establishing and maintaining positive working relationships with full-time and part-time departmental staff, support teachers, ancillary staff such as laboratory technicians, other subject leaders and members of the SMT. Therefore, in this chapter, the antithesis of teamwork is the focus of attention, i.e. the subject leader acting as a political leader. It is recognized that conflicts of opinion will occasionally arise between committed teachers. In such a context, it is more appropriate for the SL to be perceived to act as a transactional leader (Burns, 1978). This perspective emphasizes the political nature of leadership and includes negotiation and bargaining with the SMT, as well as getting departmental staff to: 'do things they don't really want to do' (O'Neill, 2000). As has already been stated, any group of professional teachers is bound to have occasional disagreements about a range of organizational and individual issues involving proposed changes to the status quo. It is worthy of note that the TTA (1998) standards for subject leaders do not specifically refer to the political task of managing conflict, but, instead, include among the skills of subject leaders, the ability to:

> deal sensitively with people, recognise individual needs, and take account of them in securing a consistent team approach to raising achievement in the subject. (p. 7)

Schmuck and Runkel (1994) expressed the view that most education professionals are unaccustomed to expressing their disagreement openly with those with whom they work most closely. This could be based on concerns that such conflicts might damage the departmental collegial climate and it is quite likely that HoDs would go to any lengths to avoid conflict. Any damage to departmental morale arising from a conflict between staff may well have an impact on departmental performance. The nature of conflict itself can vary enormously, from mild disagreement with the views of a colleague to intense disagreement, possibly relating to differences in deeply held educational values between two or more participants which might involve their emotions. Subject leaders would be well versed in coping with inter-pupil conflict but may well find themselves struggling to manage conflict between adults in such a close working environment as a department.

The meaning attached to the word 'conflict' needs to be clarified. For example, when does a disagreement become a conflict? How can it best be defined? According to Katz and Lawyer (1994), conflict could be usefully defined as:

> a situation or state between at least two independent parties, which is characterised by perceived differences that the parties evaluate as negative. (p. vii)

They argued that conflict could serve a constructive purpose, provided that the person managing the conflict is able to engage in constructive dialogue and listens carefully to what each person is saying, as well as keeping control of their own emotions.

According to Walton (1997) interpersonal conflict may be defined as including two important aspects:

> (1) substantive disagreements such as differences over objectives, structures, policies and practices and (2) the more personal and emotional differences that arise between human beings. (p. 110)

In Walton's view, it is not possible to have a conflict-free organization and he argued that some degree of conflict is healthy as it can promote innovation. In similar fashion, Everard *et al.* (2004) advocated the notion of conflict as having two components: rational and emotional. The rational element, in this context, is probably most apparent when individual members of the department argue from different perspectives in formal or informal meetings. The emotional component can be disruptive if personal 'glory' or credibility is staked on the outcome of a debate. Fullan (1993) argued very persuasively that one of the key lessons in dealing with change successfully is that 'conflict is essential to any successful change effort' (p. 27). His view is that problems are often difficult to solve, should not be avoided and new insights emerge when discussion provokes both agreement and disagreement between participants.

Following further discussion of the ideas related to power, conflict and the strategies which subject leaders might use when acting as political leaders, some research evidence will be presented which illustrates, by way of examples, different forms of conflict which subject leaders have encountered. Face to face interviews were conducted among a sample of Heads of Department working in secondary schools in Wales, as part of Phase 2 of the research.

Approaches to conflict

Any conceptualization of conflict must be situated within the broader context of what various commentators have referred to as 'micropolitics' (Hoyle 1986; Ball 1993) which, according to Hoyle (1982):

embraces those strategies by which individuals and groups in organisational contexts seek to use their resources of power and influence to further their interests. (p. 88)

What are these 'resources of power' referred to by Hoyle? The concept of power involves notions of authority and influence. Authority has the greater relevance when SLs are dealing with the Headteacher or governors, as it would be generally accepted that headteachers have the final responsibility for everything that happens in their school. Thus power is exercised in a predominantly hierarchical authoritarian sense, although this does not mean that the SL is unable to influence the thinking of the Headteacher. The authority of a subject leader can be undermined when one person (Y), working in the same department, decides to challenge X (the SL) on the grounds that Y feels that they are better suited to the job and were overlooked at interview. Subject leaders are far more likely to exert some form of influence on the ways in which the department works. By its very nature, the exercise of influence by the subject leader can be quite subtle. Two examples can be given here. One is the ability of the subject leader to influence the thinking and behaviour of departmental staff by modelling desirable characteristics and using their personality (perhaps based on charisma or sheer enthusiasm) to lead the department in a particular direction. A second example lies in the (probably subconscious) desire of those being led to identify with the leader.

Schmuck and Runkel (1994) suggested five different sources of conflict:

- Differentiation of function: differences which might arise between a departmental group who might be primarily concerned with the interests of their own area of the curriculum and members of the SMT who have to embrace a whole-school perspective and think about the interests of the school as a whole
- Power struggles: these can arise, for example, when one member of the departmental team wishes to gain an undue influence over the rest of their colleagues in terms of what should happen in a given situation

- Role conflict: this may occur if an SL does not enact their role in ways which fulfils the expectations of their line manager who might be a member of the SMT
- Differences in interpersonal style: this aspect reflects the fact that individuals in any organization work in their own unique ways within it, which can sometimes lead to conflict
- Stress: caused by changes imposed by external agents such as central government which bring about differences of opinion at the departmental level as the best way forward

Strategies for the management of conflict

Bargaining and negotiation form an important part of life for a subject leader within the political context in which they work. Blasé and Anderson (1995) suggested there were six political strategies which were used by teachers when dealing with their principals and they could apply equally well to subject leaders when they deal with other members of staff.

1. Diplomacy: SLs might use this strategy as a form of self-protection. The use of diplomatic language would be particularly important when needing to defend a contentious decision taken by the SMT or Headteacher in a departmental meeting.
2. Conformity: SLs may be able to reduce potentially harmful conflict by behaving in an appropriate manner and showing a willingness to develop departmental policies in line with whole-school policies.
3. Extra work: on occasions, SLs might well take on extra duties and responsibilities rather than delegate them to other departmental staff. Allowing someone else to take additional responsibilities runs the risk of a potential conflict if that person does not fulfil the requirements demanded of them.
4. Visibility: SLs might behave in ways designed to promote support for departmental goals from the SMT or departmental staff. This may well reduce the potential for conflict and increase consensus. For example, it might include the display of pupils' work or staff being invited to observe an innovative approach to teaching in the classroom.

5. Avoidance: SLs might act in ways which would reduce a real or perceived threat to their credibility or position from a member of the departmental team or SMT. This could involve not responding to questions or comments made in meetings about particular issues which might generate an unwarranted conflict.
6. Ingratiation: SLs may use particular tactics (for example, offer verbal support, encouragement and praise) to deliberately raise the self-esteem of departmental staff, in order to reduce potential conflict and to establish a positive working climate.

Conflict and the subject leader: some evidence from practitioners

Thirty-six subject leaders, who were interviewed in Phase 2, were asked to comment on conflict in their department. Twelve declined to comment on the ways they dealt with conflict, either stating that there was no conflict in the department or declining to make any comment about it. The reasons for this may be that the negative emotion often associated with conflict over ideas or behaviour is just too difficult for HoDs to discuss. It could also be a simple reflection of the Schmuck and Runkel position, referred to earlier, i.e. education professionals just do not like talking about conflict. Equally, the HoDs could be very skilful in conflict avoidance and have been able to engender a collegial atmosphere. Of these twelve HoDs, six were Heads of Mathematics and this could partially be explained by findings from other research (Turner, 2002 and Siskin, 1994), which indicated that there is broad agreement among Mathematics teachers about subject content and, to a lesser extent, pedagogical delivery.

An analysis of the comments made by subject leaders showed that there were five different forms of conflict which emerged from the data.

Conflict between the subject leader and the SMT or Headteacher

This could take several different forms. In the example given below, an HoD describes a proposed timetable change which the Headteacher vetoes. It shows the Headteacher exercising his positional power in the negotiations with the HoD. The HoD appears to adopt a diplomatic strategy to help defuse the potential conflict.

> If I go and say to the Headteacher, 'Next year can't we organize the timetable so that English is autonomous? We don't mind if you lump us in with humanities. We've got more in common with humanities' and I'm afraid the result is no. So I go back to the department and say 'He says no', and on the one hand that bonds us together. On the other hand, I would love to be able to come back to them and say, 'Yes, we've got what we wanted'. (Head of English)

Conflict between the HoD and one member of the departmental team

This type of conflict was the one most frequently commented upon by HoDs. It took various forms and four examples are included here for extensive discussion. In the first example, differences about pedagogy arose in relation to the teaching of a particular module. The type of conflict illustrates the different interpretations placed by the HoD and the member of the department on the value of the teaching approaches suggested in the scheme of work for a particular module. Here the HoD wanted to introduce a change to the scheme of work and he was relying on another member of staff for ideas. He did not see himself as a specialist in this area of Science. When his suggestion was rejected by a member of the departmental team, he used an avoidance strategy (Blasé and Anderson, 1995) and did not pursue a confrontation with the member of staff concerned.

> One unit relates to Year 7 which I found was incredibly boring, and so I went to one colleague and suggested that 'perhaps we ought to be doing this differently. Can you come up with some ideas?' He just looked me straight in the eye and said 'there's absolutely nothing wrong with this and I have no intention of changing it'. After some time, he did come back to me and say 'yes, you know, you are right'. We had this softly, softly approach to it. I sometimes wonder whether it might have been my approach at the time; the manner in which I asked. (Head of Science)

In the second example, differences surfaced between the views of an HoD and a member of the department in a meeting when debating the use of resources. The HoD does not appear to value the use of photocopied sheets as highly as a member of the department does. Control of resources is always a potential source of conflict in any department. Here, the HoD used a diplomatic strategy (Blasé and Anderson, 1995) when acting as a final arbiter in an attempt to solve conflict of views.

> One of the major conflicts I think is the use of resources. Limitations as far as photocopying is concerned is a major conflict. We talk about why we need to photocopy and the problem is not just one of resources, but it's also one of teaching styles. Sometimes people fall into the 'death of a thousand worksheets' trap. One of the ways of controlling that to a certain extent is by limiting photocopying. So one particular member of staff was very, very angry about the fact that I was limiting the photocopying, and that argument actually brought us around to teaching styles. He still doesn't agree with what I do but we've talked it through and it's not me and him, it's the whole department discussing it and I think that is very, very valuable. (Head of Science)

Clearly one of the positive outcomes of a discussion about the use of photocopied sheets, is a sharing of ideas about different teaching styles in the department.

In the third example, conflict occurred as a result of poor attendance by one member of departmental staff. The conflict was difficult to manage because of the sympathy felt by the HoD for the member of staff concerned and the conflict remained unresolved. The HoD was not able to directly influence or motivate the individual member of staff to change their behaviour.

> SL: I've got one person who I have had a bit of conflict with. Well, I wouldn't shout at them, but we've discussed his problems. His attendance is very poor. I mean I've tried and we've talked about it and everything and it's made no difference but then the head teacher's done exactly the same and it's made no difference. I've done it in a friendly way, but it's not going to alter.

Interviewer: So, this person sometimes just doesn't turn up?

SL: I think he is actually ill and if he's got a cold he's off for a week ... No amount of talking will make any difference at all. When he's here, he does a very good job. It's just he suffers from ill health. ... The rest of the staff complain because he's away quite often but I mean there's no point in talking because that is his nature. If he could, he would be off for weeks, so what can you do? (Head of Science)

In the fourth example, problems arose because a member of the department had previously failed to get the vacant subject leader post at interview. Here, the nature of the conflict was more subversive, leading to ongoing problems which were difficult to resolve and is a good example of the source of conflict being a power struggle between the current HoD and the previous post-holder. The HoD had to use a judicious mixture of positional power and coercive power on occasions when dealing with an awkward member of the department.

There was an acting Head of Department who held the job I applied for. He was turned down for the position so that was a particularly difficult situation. I came on a visit after my appointment and I asked to see him specifically and I immediately said 'look I know I realize it is a difficult position for you. At the end of the day, there will be things on which I will seek your advice and I will respect the fact that you have more experience in this school than I do but the other side of the coin is that I carry the can as I am the Head of Department.' I think we had a working relationship in the end but the very nature of my appointment and the fact that he was within the Department always made it slightly difficult. The thing I found was that he would try to engage people if he didn't agree with something to back him up in his arguments whereas on a one-to-one he wouldn't do that. So I would actually see him on a one-to-one basis. I would attempt to try and persuade him by going through the reasons for my doing what I was doing but there always came a time or there would come a time occasionally where you know you had to say, 'Well I'm sorry on that we will differ and I am the Head of Department'. (Head of Mathematics)

Conflict between different members of the department

An example shows the subject leader using a problem-solving approach to resolve a difficulty brought about by one member of staff wishing to change the existing rooming arrangements.

X, the Drama and English teacher, has a real problem in terms of getting space in the school. The PE Department are very good but basically you have two people competing and timetabled for the same space which can be difficult. If someone perhaps leaves chairs out and things like that that creates conflict. We had a little hiccup yesterday where X has a large Year 9 class and suddenly X realized she couldn't get her group in there and said 'can I swap rooms with Y'? Now Y is very fond of his room. Y is the second in Department and I said 'right could you swap?' He wasn't too happy but off he went and then came back and said 'there's only four desks in there and she needs another two tables in Room Z which is bigger'. I thought I know what that's about. He wants to stay in his little room at the back and get on with his Record of Achievement work which is usually the case. I then went and checked and in fact he was quite right. They were both competing for space; the only way out of it was, I swapped with X because I've got the bigger room. (Head of English)

Conflict between one member of the department and other members of the team

A Head of Science described how one member of the team had failed to complete a task on time. Here the subject leader avoided a conflict between one member of the departmental team and the rest by smoothing out the difficulty caused by this member of staff not completing a task because of lack of time.

One of the teachers said we'll do something on assessment in Year 7 and we had a meeting. He came with further proposals to change. I said 'Let's see the results now of what you've done'. Unfortunately he didn't have any results of what he'd done. He hadn't collated everything so that stopped and it could have led to a difficult situation, not between me but between other members of staff. We're not letting him go away thinking he's been totally useless. (Head of Science)

Conflict between the HoD, Headteacher and members of the departmental team

An example of conflict was given by one HoD who described how conflict arose when the Headteacher insisted on introducing a new policy of mixed-ability teaching across the school. This was discussed at a departmental meeting and this example illustrates how the subject leader could only play the role of translator and mediator of whole-school policy, rather than engage in discussion to change or challenge the policy. The HoD could only use an avoidance strategy, as the positional power over the decision-making process in this instance lies in the hands of the Headteacher.

> The head wants mixed ability, more differentiation and that is what we were talking about in the departmental meeting. So one of mine said, 'If there's any mixed-ability teaching in this school, I'll be writing to my MP.' Somebody else said 'what I'm worried about is the kid who sits in the corner and doesn't say anything and it's easy to let them get away with it'. Somebody else said 'well we've done really well in this department and our results have improved'. So I said 'okay all those things are accepted but this is the direction the head is asking us to go in, because that is what we have to do. What we have to do is to talk about how we're going to do it to our satisfaction, not whether we're doing it but how we're going to do it.' (Head of English)

What was surprising about this example was that it was taking place in an English department, which has traditionally been more favourable to mixed-ability teaching compared to a subject like Mathematics.

Conflict and the HoD: a summary

Disagreements between departmental staff are inevitable in the sense that professional teachers will not always agree with one another. Some of the examples quoted here are relatively minor in terms of their emotional impact on the HoD. Others stirred up more emotion. This is an area of the work of subject leaders which has attracted comparatively little attention, in contrast with the principles of collegial practice and teamwork which tend to underpin the TTA (1998) standards for subject leaders. However, in practice, it remains a difficult area to research because of the reluctance of subject leaders to discuss it. In the research sample used in this chapter, one third of the respondents declined to comment on the ways in which they managed conflict. Perhaps they were the ones who were able to spot potential areas of conflict and use avoidance strategies to prevent its occurrence. On occasions, a subject leader does have to act as a transactional leader (for example, negotiating with the Headteacher on behalf of the department), from a position of delegated responsibility in which the Headteacher has the ultimate authority in terms of their positional power. Clearly, the most common form of conflict occurred when SLs had to deal with individual departmental staff. Differences between the subject leader and members of the department in terms of ideological outlook were not really discussed in this research. Some forms of conflict appear to be exceedingly difficult to resolve at a departmental level, particularly concerning frequent absence of a colleague and dealing with someone who has failed to be given the Head of Department post at interview as an internal candidate. The difficulties subject leaders experienced in dealing with these issues seemed to be tied in with the extent to which the two people concerned were able to establish positive working relationships.

Future work on the micropolitical aspects of a subject leader's work may need to take account of the prevailing climate (increasingly being dominated by performance management) in which secondary schools now have to operate. According to Gunter (2001), the trend towards more site-based performance management means that:

> middle management is becoming less concerned with child welfare and more a means through which accountability is achieved. (p. 108)

This trend may well mean that there is greater potential for conflict in the future between HoDs and SMTs as well as between staff in the same department, as the expectations (usually politicians') regarding the outcomes of the education process continue to rise. These demands are accompanied by pressure from target setting for

SATs, GCSEs and other examination results. This may then lead to a greater intolerance of perceived departmental underperformance.

> **Discussion points**
> 1. Identify a conflict of opinion which has occurred in your department. Analyse it according Schmuck and Runkel's classification in terms of (a) the type of conflict it might be and (b) the source of the conflict.
> 2. Secondary schools have limited human and material resources. Identify ways in which inter-departmental conflicts of interest might best be reduced.
> 3. If conflict is a normal part of organizational life, why do subject leaders find it difficult to talk openly about it?
> 4. Your are a newly appointed, relatively young subject leader, appointed as head of a large department such as English or Mathematics. Your department contains several more experienced, older members of staff who are resistant to change, especially when it comes to discussion of the increased use of ICT in subject teaching. In such circumstances, how might any conflict of opinion be best managed? How might support from members of the SMT be utilized?
> 5. As a subject leader, one of your most important roles is to liaise with both departmental staff and the SMT. To what extent can you, as a political leader, carry out your liaison role more effectively in school?

Further reading

Ball, S. (1987) *The Micro-politics of the School: Towards a Theory of School Organisation,* London: Methuen.
Gold, A. (1998) *Head of Department: Principles in Practice,* London: Cassell.
Handy, C. (1990) *Inside Organisations,* London: Penguin Books.
Kydd, L., Anderson, L. and Newton, W. (2004) *Leading People and Teams in Education,* London: Paul Chapman.

6 The subject leader and the management of change

Introduction

The main aim of this chapter is to highlight the work of a subject leader as a change agent who might normally work with a group of departmental staff. It complements the ideas discussed in the previous two chapters on teamwork and micropolitics.

Coping with change presents the subject leader with an enormous challenge. On the one hand, he/she is a team leader and on the other, he/she is a political leader, charged with either implementing change in accordance with whole-school policy or initiating change at a departmental level, working with departmental staff who may not necessarily welcome any form of change. This is a reflection of the fact that, as James and Connolly (2000) argued, change is inextricably linked with learning and emotions. Change involves risk which can lead to uncertainty. Possibly the two greatest barriers to change facing some subject leaders are: (a) challenging an existing, traditional departmental culture with the intention of creating a new one (for example, placing a much greater emphasis on the use of ICT in lessons) and (b) dealing with the ever-present difficulties associated with lack of time (Earley and Fletcher-Campbell, 1992), bearing in mind that most subject leaders have heavy teaching commitments themselves.

Change is fundamentally linked to school improvement in the quest to raise standards in education. It is not possible to have improvement without change but it is perfectly possible to introduce change without producing the desired improvements. Indeed, according to Fullan (in Bennett *et al.*, 1992), most changes fail to deliver the expected outcomes.

Field *et al.* (2000) argue a strong case for most school-based change being incremental or evolutionary. For subject leaders, this means initiating appropriate amendments to schemes of work or discussing with departmental staff ways of introducing more formative assessment, to take account of the findings of Black and Wiliam (2002). However, it is also possible for a school to slip into 'special measures' following an inspection. In such a case as this, urgent action is required, which Field *et al.* refer to as revolutionary change. Perhaps one of the most challenging roles of the subject leader is to help staff deal with the emotional impact of change while maintaining departmental morale at the same time.

In the final part of this chapter, some case-study evidence is presented which describes the experiences of a Head of English when dealing with change (the same person who was interviewed as in Chapter 4 about team leadership).

The subject leader as a change agent

It is surprising to note that that there are no explicit references to the management of change in the TTA (1998) document relating to subject leaders. However, there are occasional references to 'improvement', mainly through the use of target-setting procedures. It may therefore be concluded that, as no improvement in standards can occur without change, the TTA document makes the assumption that subject leaders have an implicit understanding of the nature of change.

One obvious question concerns the role of the subject leader in the change process. To what extent is the subject leader a manager of change as well as a change agent? The answer may well depend on the nature of the change being advocated and the specific departmental context which exists at the time. If the innovation is being advocated at a whole-school level or being imposed as a result of changes in policy at national or LEA level, then the subject leader becomes more of a manager of change who is concerned about how best to implement the changes introduced at national, local or whole-school level (for example, the introduction of literacy strategies in KS3). However, the subject leader may also be the initiator of desirable change (as they see it) in which case, it might be more reasonable to cast their role in terms of being a change agent. What do change agents actually do? Morrison (1998) argued that:

> change agents are able to define goals that are achievable and are able to respond to changes which might lie outside the immediate field of the project in question, i.e. taking risks. (p. 221)

Harris *et al.* (1997), in their study of effective departments, found that subject leaders had a crucial role to play in establishing the right kind of climate to enable change to be acceptable. It would normally be the responsibility of the subject leader acting as the change agent who would drive the change process, from initiation to implementation. Any attempt to coerce departmental staff into a change in behaviour or attitude, however desirable, is almost certain to fail, as staff would only pay lip-service to new ways of working.

One of the key aspects of change in the present climate in which schools have to operate is that change is often managed in a top-down fashion, with little consultation with subject leaders. The subject leader may then find him/herself in the unenviable position of being forced to interpret whole-school policies, with which they might not agree, in a departmental context. Reeves *et al.* (2001) found evidence of two identifiable roles for change leaders (i.e. subject leaders acting as change agents in a leadership role). One related to the change agent having a clear understanding of the content of the innovation and a personal belief in its worth. The other related to an interest in and experience of the management and facilitation of change. Reeves *et al.* claimed that the successful introduction of change was associated with *both* roles being positively fulfilled.

One problem faced by all subject leaders is how to cope with the wave upon wave of policy initiatives imposed on schools from central government (referred to in Chapter 1). Fleming (2000) argues that this has left many teachers: 'feeling deskilled, mere technicians following the instructions of those on high' (p. 119). Thus the subject leader as a change agent has to prioritize in relation to the implementation of change as a way of protecting the subject department (particularly less experienced colleagues) from work overload.

Even if the subject leader manages to prioritize multiple changes successfully, the management of change remains problematic. For example, Gunter (2001) argues that tensions may arise when an individual subject leader wishes to introduce changes in teaching and learning strategies which conflict with the ways in which the SMT desire the subject to be taught. These tensions are the result of conflict between the subject leader acting as a change agent responsible for the implementation of whole-school policy and the subject leader being pro-active in the initiation of change in the department, based on professional judgement. Glover *et al.* (1998) argued that in general subject leaders mediate and translate whole-school policy rather create it. This may be true for areas such as assessment and discipline but the essence of departmental policy is concerned with pedagogical issues directly related to the teaching and learning in the subject.

HoDs as team leaders and the politics of change

Team leadership and the management of change appear to place the subject leader in a paradoxical position. On the one hand, the subject leader is dealing with the complexities, confusions and uncertainties that risk-taking change always brings, as well as teacher suspicion and resistance. On the other hand, the subject leader has to create a stable, confident departmental climate for all the departmental members and build consensus within a framework of teamwork.

It is possible to compare the ideas about subject leaders as team leaders (Katzenbach and Smith, 1993) and subject leaders as change agents (which is my interpretation of the work of Buchanan and Boddy (1992)). The comparison may be seen in Table 6.1 (below). There are certain characteristics of change agents which are very important according to Morrison (1998). For example, being able to take a broader holistic view when considering solutions to problems (helicoptering) and being willing to take risks when the outcome is far from certain. Also, the political dimension of being a change agent appear to be more demanding; for example, dealing with conflicts, selling ideas to some teachers who may feel very reluctant to engage in a proposed change. Therefore, it is not being advocated that these two aspects of a subject leader's job (i.e. change agency and team leadership) are in opposition but rather contrast in terms of the pressures which they bring.

The true test of the effectiveness of any team of professionals (departmental or otherwise) is how it copes when change is introduced. Teacher resistance to change is a well-documented

Table 6.1   A comparison of the skills and competencies required of a subject leader, when acting as a change agent and a team leader

Skills and competences	HoD as a change agent (following Buchanan and Boddy, 1992)	HoD as a team leader (following Katzenbach and Smith, 1993 and TTA, 1998)
Goal setting	HoD is sensitive to the perceptions and expectations of the SMT HoD is aware of the national and local agenda in terms of targets set in public examinations HoD might be prepared to take risks to achieve desirable goals	HoD can set direction and establish goals for the department HoD is willing to take the lead and be open to constructive suggestions from colleagues
Role specification	HoD is effective in liaising with the SMT and with departmental colleagues HoD can identify and bring together key people to work on the proposed change	HoD can inspire departmental team HoD can lead by example and be a role model for other staff HoD is effective in team building HoD acts with integrity HoD can delegate responsibilities and chair meetings effectively
Communication (based on good inter-personal skills)	HoD can communicate effectively to all departmental members the need for change HoD can clarify what the change will mean and explain what impact the change will have on individuals HoD can bargain effectively with departmental staff	HoD can represent the team to other HoDs, the SMT and to parents HoD can establish and communicate trust and build the confidence of team members HoD can create the opportunities for developing the leadership potential of others

Table 6.1   *(continued)*

Skills and competences	HoD as a change agent (following Buchanan and Boddy, 1992)	HoD as a team leader (following Katzenbach and Smith, 1993 and TTA, 1998)
Negotiation skills	HoD can sell ideas and communicate the vision effectively within the department HoD can negotiate for the required resources HoD can resolve conflict HoD can negotiate effectively for organizational change at the whole-school level to accommodate the departmental change	HoD can maximize available resources HoD can negotiate and consult effectively
Liaison with SMT (managing up) and departmental staff	HoD is able to work effectively within the micropolitical framework in the school HoD is able to influence departmental staff who may be resistant to the proposed change, to secure their eventual commitment HoD is able to adopt a holistic view and not be solely concerned with a narrow departmental perspective	HoD can judge when to make decisions, when to consult with others and when to defer to the SMT

phenomenon. Morrison (1998) has listed a wide range of sources of resistance to educational change. These include:

> fear of the unknown, lack of clarity of purpose, reluctance to let go of the present, threats to expertise and established skills, fear of failure and threats to self-esteem and increased workload. (p. 127–8)

Dealing with such resistance entails a great deal of patient discussion and debate with departmental colleagues on the part of the HoD.

If the reasons for the introduction of the proposed change are not made explicit and the advantages to be gained by pupils in terms of teaching and learning are not clarified, then the change will fail. Threats to expertise are very real for some teachers and the training implications for such staff should be carefully considered by the HoD. Increased workload is, to some extent, under greater scrutiny following the signing of a workload agreement between the government and most of the teaching unions in January 2003. Some of the implications of the workforce reforms are discussed in Chapter 13.

Case study evidence

Research methodology
The evidence presented here reports the views of the same Head of English (Jackie) and two members of the English department, in the same school as described in Chapter 4. It was anticipated that the two departmental staff interviewed (Sue and Alison) would be conscious of changes that had been recently introduced. The same questions (phrased appropriately) were posed to the HoD and two members of her department. This gave the opportunity for triangulation to take place in the analysis of the following comments. The insights into change came from questions relating to the methods used by HoDs to improve teaching and learning when (a) working with individuals and (b) working with the department in formal meetings. HoDs were asked how successful these methods were and which methods had been tried and found to be unsuccessful.

Findings
Changes which had been recently introduced or would be introduced
Two examples were discussed by the Head of English. The first was concerned with individual staff being encouraged to evaluate their teaching in departmental meetings. She had introduced an element of reflective evaluation among her colleagues, which she admitted had taken time to become embedded. Some of the English teachers appeared to be finding this change of approach in departmental meetings difficult to cope with.

I do encourage individuals to think reflectively about their own work because I think that is part of what we should do as professionals. I think that that is an element that is new in the department. I think sometimes they wonder why I'm asking them to consider certain questions because they're not used to using meetings for that kind of philosophical approach. They're more used to using them for the business of what needs to be done and admin. (Jackie)

Jackie's perception that self-evaluation was important was reinforced by Sue, as can be seen in the following comments:

I think our head of department, within the time restraints forced upon her, certainly encourages us to think reflectively about our teaching and I think the feedback that we receive with the exercise books for instance is part and parcel of that process.

The second example involved a recent change in departmental procedure where departmental staff were to be observed by the HoD. Observing other departmental staff teach was bound to stir up anxiety particularly as teachers may be unsure about how the information gleaned from the lesson observation might be used. Even Sue appeared to be a little 'cagey' about the process.

This is something that we are exploring at the moment. It hasn't actually taken place as yet. It's tended to be the head of department observing the department.

She had little to say about classroom observation of her teaching. However, Alison expressed more appreciation for the support and feedback which she received from her HoD. She also revealed that it had stirred up some concerns among the departmental staff.

She saw everyone teach when she first came, because obviously she wanted to have a look at what everyone was doing in their classrooms. I went in and saw her teach simply because we shared a sixth-form group and we did a sort of induction which she led. So I saw her do some work with the sixth form before she'd seen me teach. But she then did go into everyone's class-room and have a look at what they were doing, which some people found very nerve-racking. I was used to people being in and out and I found it really interesting having her there and she sort of contributed to the lesson and took part in it, so I really enjoyed that.

Interviewer: In this process did she make notes, did she give you any written feedback?

Yes she did. She made notes during the lesson and she gave me some written feedback, which was encouraging. (Alison)

Changes planned for the future
Here Jackie identified two issues which she feels are important to address, within this context of working with a department containing both experienced and inexperienced staff. Team teaching has already been mentioned in respect to the HoD working with an inexperienced English teacher in the context of A level studies.

Team teaching I think is important – I've only been here two terms so I haven't got that underway at this particular school but in the past I've thought that's important particularly when there are techniques that you want introduced which a teacher's not happy with or is feeling insecure about. (Jackie)

Boys' underachievement may well be part of a whole-school concern, but is particularly important in a subject like English, given current concerns about literacy which are outlined in detail in Maynard (2002).

The 'underachievement of boys' is on the agenda to be looked at because quite a lot of the research I've read on the subject suggests that there are certain types of tasks that boys achieve better results on and the way in which the English testing at GCSE is going, there are opportunities to develop those skills for boys, so that's something we are concerned about. (Jackie)

This would mean that the HoD might introduce changes to the schemes of work in KS3 in order to encourage boys to achieve higher standards. In addition, Alison commented on a recent departmental discussion focusing on the ways in which the curriculum might become more varied.

> We were discussing how we want to get more Welsh literature into Key Stage 3. We are looking to move forward in terms of the variety of tasks we ask children to do, and in terms then of what they get out of English – making English enjoyable – because I think probably five years ago here it was very boring. Everyone was doing comprehensions every lesson, working in silence.

Unfortunately, it was not possible to know whether the departmental staff 'bought' into the idea of making the curriculum more varied and enjoyable. This most recent development was not mentioned by either member of the department.

Changes which did not work
Here Jackie gives an example of change being unsuccessfully introduced. The tensions induced among the departmental staff by appearing to increase the demands on teacher time with more paperwork resulted in the scheme being eventually rejected by the department for possibly quite justifiable reasons.

> In the two terms here there's been something that has been unsuccessful already. That is when I first came here I wanted my staff to adopt a system which I already used in my other school which was for them to make fortnightly plans and they're quite detailed sheets because I think planning should be activity based. They contained details of activities, resources, the programmes of study they relate to, differentiation, that kind of thing. I wanted them to do them fortnightly for each class they did and they weren't happy about it. Some started off doing them and anyway I asked for them in first off, so I would know that they had done them. There were a couple of people who were very entrenched, who dug their heels in, and said that they couldn't plan that way in advance because they would change what they were going to do. ... So the fortnightly planning didn't work I think because it is hard work to do it initially and because people

weren't convinced that this was something that was going to actually improve their teaching.

She had tried to implement an innovation in her present school which had worked well in her previous school. However, she made the assumption that the departmental staff would understand the need for such a change. What she overlooked was that some of the staff did not believe the advantages associated with introducing planning sheets would outweigh the costs in changing established practice. This is an example of active resistance, where staff were obviously reluctant to change their patterns of working.

Summary

Being a change agent, either from a whole-school perspective or a departmental perspective demands a different set of skills, of which three appear to be significant. First, a sense of timing is very important because, if an innovation is introduced at the wrong time, it will be misunderstood and rejected. Secondly, the ability to motivate people to want to change their practice (because of the clearly laid out benefits it is likely to bring) is essential. Thirdly, dealing with teacher resistance in a sensitive fashion is likely to produce a positive outcome.

It is surprising to note the extent of the similarities between these important aspects of being an HoD. However, it might be postulated that an HoD cannot be an effective change agent without first being a good team leader. For example, being able to explain what a change might mean and why it might be desirable presupposes that the HoD has already established their own credibility as a teacher, is a good role model, can deal sensitively with others and resolve conflict where it arises.

It may well be that an HoD can be a good team leader but not necessarily a successful manager of change and vice versa. All this leads to a possible model, which characterizes both the subject leader and the likely outcome in terms of departmental performance (see Figure 6.1). Further research evidence will be needed to enable a judgement to be made as to whether such a model is potentially useful in describing the complementary roles of team leader and change agent, where the political skills of the subject leader become more important.

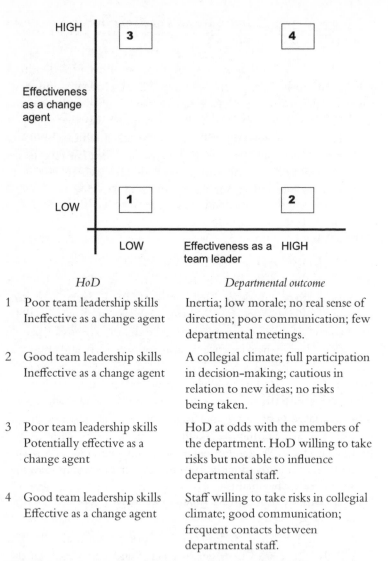

	HoD	Departmental outcome
1	Poor team leadership skills Ineffective as a change agent	Inertia; low morale; no real sense of direction; poor communication; few departmental meetings.
2	Good team leadership skills Ineffective as a change agent	A collegial climate; full participation in decision-making; cautious in relation to new ideas; no risks being taken.
3	Poor team leadership skills Potentially effective as a change agent	HoD at odds with the members of the department. HoD willing to take risks but not able to influence departmental staff.
4	Good team leadership skills Effective as a change agent	Staff willing to take risks in collegial climate; good communication; frequent contacts between departmental staff.

Figure 6.1 A comparison of the effectiveness of an HoD as a change agent and team leader in relation to departmental outcomes

Discussion points and practical activities
1. Reflect on an example of change which has been introduced recently. Do your departmental colleagues understand

the reasons for the change? In what ways has it added to the workload? How have you dealt with any teacher resistance?

2. Implementing any kind of change can often present the subject leader with a number of problems. Changes can be associated with the curriculum, assessment, behaviour management, target setting, monitoring, the introduction of ICT, etc. Choose one from this list or one of your choosing relating to a change which has been recently introduced. What problems arose and how were they best overcome?

3. Subject leaders often have to deal with multiple changes. How might these changes be prioritized? What criteria might be used to decide these priorities?

4. Examine Figure 6.1. Are you more effective as a team leader or as a change agent? Why might that be?

5. Interview a member of the SMT about a change which has been recently introduced at a whole-school level. Find out as much as you can about the problems which arose during the initiation and implementation phases, and how those problems were overcome.

Further reading

Altrichter, H. and Elliott, J. (2000) *Images of Educational Change*, Buckingham: Open University Press.

Busher, H. (2002) 'Managing change to improve learning' in Bush, T. and Bell, L. (eds) *The Principles and Practice of Educational Management*, London: Paul Chapman.

Day, C., Harris, A., Hadfield, M., Tolley, H. and Beresford, J. (2000) *Leading Schools in Times of Change*, Buckingham: Open University Press.

Everard, B., Morris, G. and Wilson, I. (2004) *Effective School Management*, London: Paul Chapman.

Fullan, M. (1996) *The New Meaning of Educational Change*, London: Cassell.

Fullan, M. (2003) *Change Forces with a Vengeance*, London: RoutledgeFalmer.

Macbeath, J. and Mortimore, P. (2001) *Improving School Effectiveness*, Buckingham: Open University Press.

Wallace, M. and Pocklington, K. (2002) *Managing Complex Educational Change*, London: RoutledgeFalmer.

7 The subject leader, strategic management and departmental planning

Introduction

The planning process is about translating strategy into realizable specific goals and should specify the actions which ought to occur. It is a challenging proposition to ask subject leaders both to think and plan strategically. This is because so much of what actually happens at a departmental level has to be concerned with the daily reality of task prioritization and departmental maintenance. Problems with staffing and deployment of resources often distract from the processes of strategic planning. Also, the likelihood is that performance management will dictate strategy at a departmental level. This is because whole-school targets such as improvements in pupil performance will need to be translated at a subject-department level. Nevertheless, the opportunity afforded to schools in England to become specialists in a given area of the curriculum has given greater impetus to the planning and development cycle.

It is the intention in this chapter to consider those aspects of strategic planning relevant to HoDs, departmental reviews and the limitations of strategic planning.

Useful background ideas about strategic planning

In general terms, 'strategy' may be conceived as being concerned with identifying medium to long-term goals within an organization and outlining a plan which indicates how they might be achieved. The stimulus for the creation of a strategy may well derive from a recent inspection report or changes in national educational policy which attempt to have an influence on practice at classroom level.

Strategic management consists of a number of components including reflecting, planning and evaluation. As a process, it can be an important part of the overall leadership and management functions of a subject leader, which are described in a slightly amended version of Fidler's (1997) model in Figure 7.1. This describes a one or two-year cycle when strategic plans can be drawn up, monitored, reviewed and evaluated in the light of experience and changing priorities.

There are two elements of this model which are worthy of specific mention at this point. The first is external relations which needs to be considered carefully by a subject leader if, for example, he/she is

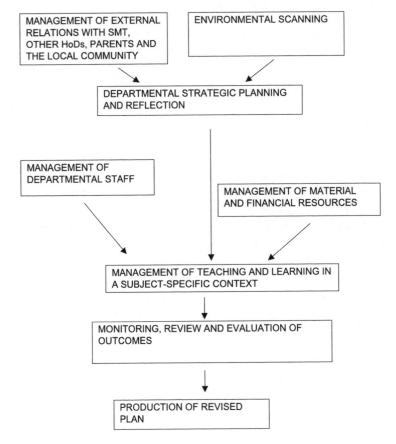

Figure 7.1   Strategic management and its relationship to other managerial activities from a departmental perspective

considering the introduction of new examination courses at the expense of more traditional ones. Time needs to be set aside in departmental meetings for the proposed change to be fully discussed among the staff so they feel some sense of ownership and can become committed to the change. The benefits of making such a change need to be carefully marketed to both pupils and their parents. The second is environmental scanning which can mean reviewing departmental policies in the light of changes to whole-school policies. It can also involve the regular scrutiny of data about pupil performance in Key Stages 3 and 4 as well as obtaining an accurate picture of the likely intake to the school from the feeder primary schools in the forthcoming year.

The management of departmental staff is considered in different ways: in Chapter 4, in the sense of managing the team; in Chapter 5, the HoD managing the micropolitics; and in Chapter 6, the HoD is perceived as either an initiator of change or the person responsible for implementing whole-school change at a subject level.

Planning takes place in secondary schools at different levels. Most schools regularly engage in some form of review and evaluation on an annual basis. Periodically, a whole-school inspection will provide some independent evidence of aspects of a school's performance which might be improved. The SMT might also engage in some form of departmental or faculty review, to monitor progress and assist in the production of improvement plans.

At the department level, HoDs might carry out some form of internal monitoring with the intention of finding out what progress the department itself is making and where the weaknesses might be. This might occur as a standing item on the agenda of a departmental meeting. All this information can facilitate the production of a development plan which might be framed over a two-year period. Such a plan will set out aims and objectives before stating clearly what the action points might be in terms of the whole curriculum, learning resources, organization and management from a whole-school perspective.

The planning documentation can also include a substantial section outlining what the departmental goals are, how they might be achieved and who might be responsible for seeing that such targets are being addressed. In addition, school-development planning of this sort will specify the success criteria to be used to judge whether such targets have been met. The context in which the school is operating also needs to be considered. A school in special measures following an inspection may well approach the whole process of strategic planning very differently from a school with a good inspection report.

I would argue that strategic thinking is about long-term planning from a whole-school perspective. However, the subject leader is usually more concerned with the implementation of strategy at the departmental level than with the creation of a whole-school plan. This raises questions about the extent to which subject leaders can play a part in whole-school policy-making and decision-making.

Earley (1998) is of the opinion that the involvement of the subject leader depends on at least three key factors: the structure of the organization (i.e. is it strongly hierarchical?); the management style of the SMT and the culture of the school (how things are done and the expectations of staff). It is most likely that planning at the departmental level is more concerned with short-term tactical procedures rather than longer-term strategic planning, despite the exhortations in the TTA (1998) standards for subject leaders to set 'long-term plans for the development and resourcing of the subject' (p. 10). This is because the pressures from the SMT and parents for subject teachers to perform and pupils to achieve acceptable examination results far outweigh any other considerations.

Field *et al.* (2000) discussed the need to develop departmental policies in line with school policies which can generate a sense of collective responsibility and provide a climate of security and stability. Evidence gleaned from the work done by Brown *et al.* (2000) appears to indicate that the extent to which departmental development plans matched school-development plans was either not known or very tenuous. However, this may well change as performance management becomes more embedded in normal practice, as it demands a close link between whole-school and departmental plans.

Strategic planning model relevant to subject leaders

A useful planning model has been suggested by Field *et al.* (2000, p. 85) and is shown in Table 7.1 in a modified form. I have included some additional comments on each of the stages outlined in Table 7.1.

Table 7.1   A useful model of the planning process relevant to HoDs

Stage	Detail	Departmental Actions
1	Establishing our purposes/goals and our values	Discussion in meetings
2	Articulating, sharing and building our vision	Discussion in meetings
3	Defining our end results	Discussion in meetings
4	Deciding what we want pupils to achieve	Setting targets in the light of whole-school targets
5	Deciding what we want staff and others to do	Discussion in meetings
6	Analysing our performance and our environment	Audit
7	Prioritizing our actions	
8	Planning for change	
9	Monitoring, evaluating and reviewing performance	Collecting and analysing evidence, e.g. through lesson observation, collecting data
10	Reporting to the stakeholders, i.e. pupils, parents, SMT and governors	

Stage 1

The subject leader can influence the departmental culture to some extent, by modelling desirable characteristics such as openness, being willing to share ideas and exhibiting trust in colleagues. However, if the prevailing culture in the school is one of mainly dealing with short-term crises, it is unlikely that strategic planning will play much part in the development of high-quality teaching and learning in the department.

Stage 2

Strategic planning involves a mix of conceptual ideas: namely vision, mission, values, beliefs and emotions. Vision might be interpreted as 'what will the future look like?'; mission can be perceived to be 'how will we get to where we want to be?'; values and beliefs incorporate what teachers believe about the purposes of education (for example, making the most of the talents of an individual pupil, giving all pupils the opportunity to develop their skills and interests); emotions, because any form of planning will want to maintain emotional stability within the organization for it to continue to thrive.

A young, inexperienced SL working with older, more experienced staff is likely to find that it might be very challenging to reach consensus on the use of ICT in the teaching of the subject in comparison to an experienced SL finding themselves working alongside several NQTs. It is quite likely that the process of building a shared vision for the teaching of the subject may well be easier in some subjects than others. Evidence to be cited in Chapter 8 indicates that teachers of Mathematics share more in the way of common perceptions of what mathematics is and how it should be taught in comparison to teachers of English, who might place greater emphasis on poetry or Shakespeare or drama.

Stage 3

The emphasis here is on outcomes, which are a reflection of statements which the HoD and departmental staff alike can draw up and discuss. According to Field *et al.* (2000, p. 101), they focus on questions such as 'What do we want the subject to be like, once we have got things the way we want them to be?' and 'When we have achieved our goals, what is it that pupils will be doing?'

Stage 4

This can be partly reflected in targets for results in examinations but it can also relate to discussions in the department about we want pupils to be able to do and/or skills we want them to be able to acquire as they gradually develop their learning capability.

Stage 5

This is obviously linked to the vision discussed earlier in Stage 2. The formulation of objectives and the ability of staff to realize those objectives in practice can be very challenging for subject leaders. This is especially true if there is an expectation that teachers will be expected to change the ways in which they teach. The subject leader may have to engage in one to one coaching or arrange for intensive training to be available for the staff involved. In my opinion, if teachers are not clear about what they need to do and also understand the reasons for doing it, then there is little chance of the vision becoming a reality.

Stage 6

This stage can include carrying out an audit of provision; comparing the performance of pupils in other comparable subjects in the school; and comparing the performance of pupils in your school with other comparable schools (benchmarking).

The audit really establishes a baseline but, arguably, the most important part is to decide the departmental goals for the subject. PM has tended to dictate that these goals are congruent with whole-school priorities; for example, raising the educational standards achieved by boys. Busher and Harris (2000, p.159) suggest what areas an audit might focus upon and an amended version of their proposal is shown in Table 7.2.

Stage 7

This process of prioritization is governed by the responses to questions which the HoD might wish to discuss with the department, in terms of the current strengths and weaknesses fundamentally related to teaching and learning in the subject. However, the subject leader may also find their priorities can change depending on whether some new whole-school innovation is advocated by the SMT who then wish to see it being implemented rapidly.

Stage 8

Having decided the subject priorities for the next year, various forms of change will need to be introduced to bring about the desired improvements. Field *et al.* (2000, p. 126) suggest that changes might be contemplated in planning (e.g. schemes of work); classroom arrangements (e.g. positioning of tables); lesson delivery (e.g. use of different teaching styles); learning activity (e.g. more use of active learning strategies); assessment (e.g. homework).

Table 7.2   Suggestions as to what might be included in a departmental audit

Aspects to be audited	Detail
Whole-school context	Basic information about the school; contact ratios for staff; annual budgets and current funding streams; pupil profiles (to include gender, ethnicity, ESL, school meals and social class); staff profiles; unit costs per student per group.
Departmental context	The extent to which departmental developments fit with whole-school developments; departmental safety issues; application of the whole-school policy on, for example, pupil behaviour in the department.
Subject concerns	Usefulness of current specifications being used at GCSE and A level; provision for SEN pupils; use of classroom assistants; pupils' achievements in public examinations; variety of teaching styles used to match pupils' learning styles.
Operations	Effectiveness of departmental meetings and the participation of staff; use of available accommodation; resources allocation to pupils and to the topics being taught; decision-making processes.
People	Relationships with staff, parents and pupils; CPD opportunities for staff; extent to which staff are hitting their PM targets; job descriptions and actual functions; pupil groupings and equality of opportunity; social activities.
Culture	Displays of pupils' work; expectations in regard to pupil behaviour and assessment of work.

Stage 9
Monitoring is a very important part of the quality-assurance process. It is primarily an ongoing process. It can include work sampling, interviews with individual staff, lesson observation, analysis of test and examination results to ensure that pupils are achieving, at the very least, what might be expected of them on the basis of past performance and data from standardized tests such as CATs scores.

Stage 10
Teachers have always been accountable to the SMT, governors and parents for the performance of pupils in their subject area but never more so than at the present time. The HoD will have to justify the progress made within the subject on an annual basis to all relevant stakeholders.

Subject development plans

Busher and Harris (2000) argued that subject or departmental development plans (DPPs) should include the following aspects:

- the curriculum
- human relations processes and values
- staff development
- decision-making and resource allocation
- links with external contexts (p. 157)

The external contexts mentioned here include the influences of the parents, local community and governors. Changes may need to be focused on: the curriculum in terms of the specification used; the introduction of more innovative teaching and learning processes; addressing staff-training needs following a needs-analysis process; thinking more about how staff and material resources might be used to best effect; utilizing expertise in the local community to enrich the curriculum experience of the pupils (for example, a parent working in the electronics industry might be asked to come into the school to present one or two aspects of their work to a group of pupils studying the subject, followed up by a reciprocal visit to the workplace to see the ideas in action).

More recent examples indicate that HoDs need to consider the following points when drawing up subject development plans: links to previous departmental development plans; staff-development review from the previous year; strategic direction planning; strategies for action; costings; individual staff-development plans.

The strategies for action should normally include the following eight aspects:

1. Key developmental issues to be addressed: these can relate to those five priorities drawn up as part of the planning process
2. Actions needed: these would focus on the specific details which have to be addressed for successful implementation
3. Persons responsible: the HoD would be expected to take a leading part in the development of new ideas in the subject. However, such actions can also be delegated to other members of staff as appropriate
4. A target completion date: this would be advisable taking into account the prevailing departmental circumstances
5. Costings: such detail would inevitably involve some form of prioritization if the departmental resources are limited
6. INSET needs: these can be addressed by arranging for staff to attend in-house training or allowing staff to participate in externally run courses
7. Monitoring procedures: the HoD could include discussion of the progress being made towards the targets identified at the regular departmental staff meetings
8. Outcome/Target: such targets should be quantifiable and would normally be linked to specific percentage figure grade A*–C at GCSE level or a percentage figure for the achievement of Level 5 in the subject (e.g. English) in Key Stage National tests

The DPP would include financial details of the income and planned expenditure to assure the SMT that spending plans can be met within existing or expected budgets.

The training issues also need to be addressed and the DPP can include details of how this will happen. They might be outlined under six headings:

- The key issues to be costed, as mentioned in 1 above
- Nature of the training needed, which can specify what course(s) will be attended

- Staff involved, which allows the training to be provided across the department
- Number of days involved in the training
- Actual cost
- Training provider can be specified

Departmental reviews

Departmental reviews can occur once a year or even once every six months. They form an integral part of the overall monitoring strategy. The review process can consist of three components:

- The subject leader is likely to be most concerned about strategic management when an annual review is carried out within the department. This can start by reviewing the existing departmental planning process (DPP) to outline what has been achieved and what remains to be developed in the coming year. This might focus on the development of key skills (for example, ICT/Numeracy/Literacy) at different stages (in Key Stage 3) or more attention could be paid to learning styles in KS3 to help learner attainment.
- It can focus on a review of staff development. It can examine whether training targets are being/have been met and evaluate the effectiveness of CPD from the viewpoint of a departmental member of staff.
- Strategic departmental planning: this process can involve setting up to five priority areas for development in the forthcoming two years with the express purpose of raising the standard of achievement. This could include, for example, more use of the IWB to develop visually based learning or more use of formative assessment in KS3 and KS4 giving more emphasis to the comments made by teachers advising pupils how they can improve the quality of their work. In order to help raise achievement, a subject leader can challenge staff to examine the existing levels of pupil achievement and, in departmental discussions, formulate new ideas about improvement strategies to be adopted. These can apply to KS3, 4 and 5.

The limitations on strategic planning facing subject leaders

Subject leaders have to operate in a turbulent, non-static environment. They can face many practical difficulties due to budgetary constraints, changes in staffing, coping with the long-term absence of a colleague, occasional difficulties with accommodation and unexpected policy initiatives (for example, changes to a section of the curriculum) which can sometimes require urgent attention.

There can also be a problem with individual members of the department holding a range of views and attitudes towards the vision for the teaching and learning in the subject which is being built, shared and articulated. According to Lumby (2003) these attitudes can range from commitment at one end of a continuum to apathy at the other.

Creating a climate in which every colleague can feel a sense of ownership can be a very challenging task. Strategic planning makes the assumption that all members of the department are working towards the same goals. However, staff leave for a variety of reasons and their replacements may not be aware of goals agreed several years ago. There is also the danger that departmental policies can be drawn up in such a way as to straitjacket staff while trying to ensure consistency throughout the department. Such a scenario can lead to a stifling of creativity which may inhibit teaching and learning in the subject.

The impact of strategic planning on the quality of teaching and learning is very difficult to ascertain. It may be possible to find an indirect link between SP and the introduction of the Key Stage 3 strategy but it would be almost impossible to *prove* a causal link between the introduction of the strategy and an improvement in KS3 SAT results. For example, in a given school, the pupils may have done better than similar groups in previous years because the pupils have been taught more effectively and there has been less staff absence.

The plans will inevitably reflect the existing state of the subject in relation to teaching and learning. A struggling department, which might be characterized by very inexperienced staff, having access to very limited resources and only achieving very modest examination results, may well focus on Ofsted criteria to try and improve standards. These might include examining current levels of pupil achievement and comparing their results with national averages and local benchmarks for the subject. The HoD may decide to focus on how well pupils understand the assessment process and whether they understand what they have to do to improve. A high-performing department may wish to try and develop more sophisticated teaching strategies: for example, greater use of ICT; giving more targeted attention to the gifted and talented pupils. Any departmental plan should focus on curriculum development, improving CPD, efficient and effective use of resources.

The final point is really a balancing act as it is very difficult simultaneously to achieve efficiency and effectiveness. This is partly because different groups of pupils make different demands on the available resources.

Example from practice

It is normal practice for each department to produce subject development plans as their contribution to the overall School Development Plan. I have included an example of a departmental development plan for a Mathematics faculty. This includes a review section dealing with the previous year's plan indicating progress made to date (see Table 7.3); a planning sheet setting new targets for the forthcoming year (see Table 7.4); and the final section dealing with staff development needs for the department (see Table 7.5).

Table 7.3 Review from previous year

Target	Examples of Tasks	Fully in place	Partly in place with improvement needed	Not in place + comments	Details of progress being made
Raising achievement at Key Stages 3, 4, and 5	• Further develop teaching activities: e.g. starters, plenaries, main activities, thinking skills tasks, exemplar lesson plans • Share good practice		✓		Mutual observations within the faculty with a focus on starters and plenaries Follow-up by sharing ideas at faculty meetings
Enhancing learning by the use of ICT	• Develop lessons using laptops and projectors + whiteboard • Revision materials on website		✓		Software to be purchased to use on laptops Revision materials on website not done yet
Contribution to literacy, numeracy and thinking skills	• Develop thinking skills and numeracy • Implement strategies discussed on literacy INSET day		✓		Literacy strategies to be implemented by the end of year
Enriching students' broader experience	• Organize: • Year 7 trip to Techniquest • Year 8 Maths circus and trail		✓		Year 7 trip booked Year 8 Mathematics circus date to be agreed for the Summer Term

Table 7.4 Planning sheet for current year

Key issue	Departmental target (outcome)	Actions needed to enable targets to be achieved	Date of achievement	Staff responsible	Resources	Examples of monitoring procedures	Success criteria
Raising achievement at Key Stage 3	79 per cent level 5+ 26 per cent level 7+	4 extra support lessons per week for Year 9 to be established	Summer of the year	Named staff	INSET time to research and design thinking skills tasks	Review data obtained from pupils performance in tests	Targets achieved
Enhancing learning by the use of ICT	Two laptop activities developed	Further developments of lessons using laptops and projectors	Summer of year	Named staff	INSET time for staff to develop tasks	Lesson observation of staff using these activities	Targets achieved
Contribution to literacy, numeracy and thinking skills	Numeracy and thinking skills to help raise standards	Revisit literacy strategies	Summer of year	Named staff	Faculty time to revisit ideas	Discussion in departmental meetings	Targets achieved
Enriching students broader experience	Organize Year 7 Techniquest trip Organize Year 9 Masterclass	Trips organized	Summer of year	Named staff	Staff released to supervise trips	Check to see if trips have been organized	Trips to take place

Table 7.5 Staff development needs

Target	INSET activity	Staff involved	Cost	Success criteria
1. 4 extra support lessons per week for Year 9	INSET time for staff to develop tasks	Named teachers	Costs included	Improved results in KS3
2. Further developments of lessons using laptops and projectors	Whole-faculty training	Named staff	Costs included	Improved results at all key stages
3. Numeracy and thinking skills	Faculty time to revisit ideas	All departmental staff	Costs included	Improved results
4. Trips organized	Staff released to supervise trips	All departmental staff	Costs included	All places filled on trips

Discussion points

1. Identify three key areas in your subject which need to be addressed in the coming year. To what extent are they directly related to raising pupil achievement?
2. What training needs have been identified for departmental staff to help address the key areas highlighted in 1. To what extent can they be met in school? How will you monitor whether the training received has had any real impact on classroom teaching and learning?
3. To what extent do departmental staff agree that the three key areas noted in 1 are the priorities for the coming year? Have they been discussed in departmental meetings?
4. As an HoD, which of the areas outlined in Table 7.2 would most benefit from a departmental audit at the present time and why?
5. Revisit your departmental development plans (DPP). To what extent are they the subject of ongoing discussion in your departmental meetings? How frequently is your subject department reviewed and how effective is the monitoring process which checks progress towards the targets stated in the DPP?

Further reading

Bell, L. (2003) 'Strategic planning in education: a critical perspective' in Davies, B. and West-Burnham, J. (eds) *Handbook of Educational Leadership and Management,* London: Pearson Education.

Caldwell, B. J. and Spinks, J. M. (1992) *Leading the Self-Managing School,* London: Falmer Press.

Davies, B. and Ellison, L. (2003) *The New Strategic Direction and Development of the School,* London: RoutledgeFalmer.

Leask, M. and Terrell, I. (1997) *Development Planning and School Improvement for Middle Managers,* London: Kogan Page.

Preedy, M., Glatter, R. and Wise, C. (2003) *Strategic Leadership and Educational Improvement,* London: Paul Chapman.

Ruding, E. (2000) *Middle Management in Action: Practical Approaches to School Improvement,* London: RoutledgeFalmer.

8 Managing a subject

Introduction

In this chapter I want to explore the ways in which the characteristics of a subject might impact on the work of subject leaders as they seek to manage the quality of classroom teaching and learning. The TTA (1998) standards for subject leaders, referred to earlier in Chapter 1, make a number of important assumptions, which, in my view, are questionable. In particular, the standards do not appear to consider that the work of subject leaders might be influenced to some degree by the nature of the subject being taught. It is accepted that the TTA standards were intended to be generic but there may well be important differences between subjects themselves which would lead subject leaders to try to manage classroom teaching and learning in a variety of different ways.

The latter part of this chapter discusses the findings from some research carried out among HoDs (originally reported in Turner, 2002 and Bolam and Turner, 1999) about the distinctive nature of four curriculum areas (English, Mathematics, Science and Technology) and the implications for teaching and learning in these subjects.

Background

Ideas about subject distinctiveness can be based on three dimensions: the *context* in which the subject is taught, i.e. subject departments which are important organizational sub-units in secondary schools; the *subject* itself, which forms a part of the overall curriculum experienced by pupils; and the HoDs as *teachers*, who are recruited on the basis of being subject specialists by virtue of their qualifications.

The working context: the subject department

Busher and Harris (2000) have conceptualized five different types of department in terms of their structure and function. They argued that English and Mathematics are 'unitary' subject departments, where the leadership and management functions can be shared among their members. The unitary nature of these departments arises because they only deal with one subject and there is a much higher likelihood of shared values among the departmental staff.

The same authors described subjects such as Technology as 'confederate', since they usually have a weak centre and powerful sub-domains, which collaborate over resources. Modern Languages departments can usually be considered to be confederate. Wise (2000) made the important point that the legitimization of the HoD's position comes from an acceptance by the group members that she/he possesses proven expertise in teaching the subject. This can be difficult to establish in confederate departments covering a broad range of subjects. She concluded that the HoD is more likely to work in a coordinating role with other teachers in the department, where she/he does not have recognized subject expertise. This led Wise to speculate that the exercise of power (in terms of influence) is more likely to be limited because of a lack of subject expertise and maybe an absence of shared values.

According to Busher and Harris (2000), 'federate' subject departments like Science tend to have a strong centre and integrated sub-domains. The degree of influence exerted by the Head of Science varied across the three Science subjects. Two other types of department can be mentioned briefly here. Busher and Harris (2000) suggested that 'impacted' departments (such as Music, Geography and History) are usually quite small in size and are single subjects in their own right. They described subjects such as ICT as 'diffuse' as they are taught across subject areas in different classrooms. Table 8.1 summarizes the ideas of Busher and Harris about subject departments.

The Subject

The fact that subjects are different from each other is axiomatic. The nature of the subject itself can influence the ways in which the job of being an HoD is implemented (Bolam and Turner, 1999), but it is less clear how these differences might influence the ways in which HoDs try to affect the quality of classroom practice. For example, a subject

Table 8.1   Types of subject department (according to Busher and Harris, 2000)

Type of department	Examples	Features
Unitary	English, Mathematics	Single subject
Confederate	Technology, Humanities, Modern Languages	Weak centre with linked subjects holding their own powerful positions
Federate	Science	Strong centre with integrated sub-subjects
Impacted	Music, History, Geography	Single subject but small in size
Diffuse	ICT	Taught across subjects in different rooms

like Mathematics is dominated by knowledge and understanding and, to a lesser extent, by skills. The advent of the National Curriculum did little to challenge the existing consensus of what the Mathematics curriculum actually is, other than introduce an attainment target (currently called 'Using and Applying Mathematics' in both England and Wales – see, for example, ACCAC, 2000) which encourages pupils to use a skills-based approach to real-life problems. According to Saunders and Warburton in Helsby and McCulloch (1997):

> Maths teachers seem imbued with a consensus on what the maths curriculum is and how it is distinguished from other areas of the curriculum. (p. 79)

This may be due to the fact that some teachers in subjects like Mathematics perceive themselves as 'subject specialists, with a narrowly defined set of responsibilities' (Turner and Bolam, 1998, p. 385, citing the work of Bennett, 1995).

In contrast, a subject like English is based mainly on the skills of reading, writing, listening and speaking and, to a lesser extent, on knowledge and understanding. There are many ways in which these skills may be practised and developed; for example, using written texts such as stories, plays, newspapers, poetry, etc. This leads to the possibility that what counts as good practice in the teaching of English might be a matter of continuous debate. Achieving internal consistency among English teachers might therefore be more challenging for Heads of English than Heads of Mathematics.

Design and Technology (henceforward known as Technology) is a hybrid subject incorporating work with food, textiles, resistant materials, systems and control and graphical products. According to Paechter (2000), government attempts to make the subject more academic by making it compulsory in the past and having an increased emphasis on design, failed to raise the status of the subject within secondary schools. Nevertheless, Technology departments employ relatively large numbers of staff in secondary schools and are comparable in size to the core subject departments.

HoDs as Subject Teachers

HoDs are usually appointed on the basis of their track record as a successful classroom practitioner and their potential ability to lead a department. Sometimes, staff are appointed who have already demonstrated their abilities as a 'second-in-the-department', often in another school. According to Gold (1998) HoDs begin with knowledge of one set of skills (associated with classroom teaching) and then develop a different set, which encompasses managing and leading a department. In unitary subjects (e.g. English and Mathematics), the HoD would almost certainly be an acknowledged expert in both subject knowledge and pedagogy. S/he would manage a team of specialists having similar backgrounds and qualifications, but they may well possess varying degrees of experience in the teaching of the subject.

This situation would not be repeated in 'federate' subjects such as Science, where individual specialists would normally teach Physics or Chemistry or Biology modules, especially to older pupils. Thus the Head of Science, who might be a Biologist by training, would defer to the Head of Physics, as Bennett (1995) argued, on 'matters of content and approach' (p. 103). Thus Heads of Science may well work to improve teaching and learning in different ways to Heads of Mathematics as the common denominator of subject background may be missing.

Evidence about subject distinctiveness

In Phase 1 of my work, subject leaders in four subject areas (Science, Mathematics, English and Technology) were asked about the distinctive features, if any, of their subject as a discipline within the National Curriculum and how those features affected teaching and learning in their subject. An assumption was made that SLs would have some knowledge of working cultures in other departments. It is unlikely that this knowledge exists in anything other than a rudimentary form. According to Becher (1989), time is more likely to be spent being socialized into the academic tribe (i.e. subject department) and defending its boundaries rather than acquiring knowledge of how other tribes survive.

In Phase 2 (reported in Bolam and Turner, 1999), SLs were asked about their perceptions of the distinctive nature of the subject (for which they were responsible) and its influence on how they worked in the department. To focus the comments of HoDs about the distinctiveness of their subject, they were provided with a check-list of possible organizational, curricular and pedagogical issues which *complemented* the ideas gleaned from Phase 1 of the research. The categories used were:

- status within the National Curriculum
- a requirement for special facilities
- reliance placed on cumulative knowledge
- the appeal of the subject to boys and girls
- timetable restrictions and/or deployment of staff
- availability of resources/materials
- use of unique methods of teaching

When discussing the results of this research, the following abbreviations will be used: HoE for Head of English; HoM for Head of Mathematics; HoS for Head of Science; and HoT for Head of Technology.

Heads of English

A total of five themes emerged from an analysis of the interview data, which can be seen in Table 8.2. Being a core subject meant that subject leaders felt they were working in the limelight at all times.

Table 8.2 The distinctive features of English as a subject and their implications for teaching and learning

Subject: English Distinctive features	Further comments and implications for teaching and learning
A core subject within the National Curriculum	In Phase 1, some of the HoEs considered that the status and consequent importance of English derived from its existence as a core subject within the National Curriculum. In Phase 2, several HoEs felt that the status of English could be a 'two-edged sword'. There was little difficulty selling the subject to the pupils (and parents) but, at the same time, the issue of accountability was never far from their minds. As one HoE put it: 'Because of the status of English in the National Curriculum, you're under the spotlight all the time.'
A skills-based subject	Some HoEs felt that English could be regarded as having a lack of content and was much more a skills-based rather than content-based curriculum (Phase 1). There was a general recognition that the acquisition of skills was a long and difficult process. Learning in English was considered to be incremental rather than sequential. One HoE felt that high attendance was a crucial factor as the acquisition of skills was dependent on a succession of lessons (for example, when studying a play). Several HoEs felt that there was the lack of a defined progression of knowledge of the subject. They considered that the subject could not be deconstructed into simple discrete elements. In their view, this affected teaching and learning in that both care and attention were needed on the part of the teacher to identify the particular needs of the individual as well as the class.

Table 8.2 (*continued*)

The cross-curricular nature of English as a subject	Some of the HoEs felt that the skills needed in English were cross-curricular with a particular emphasis on literacy and oracy (Phase 1). A variety of views were expressed in terms of the effects on teaching and learning, including the implementation of a whole-school policy on Language across the curriculum; the need to foster links across subjects; and the need to make a good case for resources/staffing/learning support.
The underachievement of boys	In Phase 2, all the HoEs interviewed commented on the underachievement of boys and the necessity of ensuring that the subject appealed equally to both sexes, which has important pedagogical implications. Several commented on the efforts which they had made to use reading material which would appeal more to boys. However, one HoE did feel that: 'as a department here we've tended probably to go too far in the direction of trying to make everything of interest to the boys, because they tend to be generally more disaffected than the girls'.
The availability of resources	A variety of opinions were expressed by HoEs in regard to the availability of resources in Phase 2. For some, it was not a distinctive feature of their subject. However, according to one HoE: 'I don't think you ever have enough, we'd like more. We'd like to have more ICT resources and materials and it certainly does affect what you do in the classroom.' Another HoE felt that this was a very important issue: 'Resources are a huge problem. Next year, 76 young people have opted to do English A level. That creates incredible stresses on the timetable and on just the sheer resources of having to cater for them.'

Table 8.3 The distinctive features of Mathematics as a subject and their implications for teaching and learning

Subject: Mathematics Distinctive features	Further comments and implications for teaching and learning
A core subject within the National Curriculum	A few HoMs noted that Mathematics was a high-profile core subject which meant there was a lot of pressure to perform well at GCSE (Phase 1). In Phase 2, all the HoMs interviewed recognized the importance of Mathematics as a core subject. In contrast to English, the 'double-edged sword' was perceived by one HoM as: 'you've got two opposing forces there if you like; high status within the National Curriculum so there are high expectations, balanced by the fact that the pupils are coming to us with not very good basic knowledge'.
A content-driven subject	Many of the HoMs felt that Mathematics was a subject which was content-driven and involved a prescriptive set of parameters to work from as well as emphasizing logical thinking (Phase 1). The implications for teaching and learning were that the pupils could be encouraged to tackle problems in a step-by-step fashion, tailored to the needs of individuals. One HoM felt that individual work schemes could be produced implying that pupils might spend more time learning on their own.
The cross-curricular nature of numeracy skills	Several HoMs felt that Mathematics provided the cross-curricular numeracy skills for use in other areas (Phase 1). One HoM commented: 'pupils need to know when and where to apply specific skills. It is a hierarchical subject needing careful building blocks to succeed. The teacher needs to put over the skills/concepts necessary. The pupils need to experience Mathematics in a variety of different contexts. They cannot progress unless the 'first' concepts are fully understood and there is a need to return to topics repeatedly with certain pupils.'

Table 8.3 (*continued*)

The underachievement of boys	Almost all the HoMs interviewed commented at length on the need to ensure that the subject appealed equally to boys and girls. However, they tended to focus more on possible reasons for the underachievement of boys, rather than the appeal of the subject. One HoM noted that, in his view, boys were more demanding on teacher time than girls and that boys responded better to practical activities.
Reliance on cumulative knowledge	In Phase 2, a reliance on cumulative knowledge was considered to be of some importance by some of the HoMs. One noted that for some pupils: 'their learning is hampered almost by their lack of ability to retain cumulative knowledge'. In addition, one other HoM considered the pupils' low standards of achievement in Mathematics on entry to that particular school (i.e. levels 2 or 3 in the National Curriculum) had a 'knock-on' effect for the Mathematics teachers.
Mathematics, Attainment Target 1	A few HoMs commented on Mathematics, attainment target 1. This is primarily assessed by means of investigations and has given pupils the freedom to do their own piece of work (Phase 1). The implications for teaching and learning were reported by one HoM as: 'placing considerable emphasis on self-belief and self-reliance on pupils through investigations and problems. Practical work involving space, shape and measure is used as often as possible.'

The skills basis of the subject was perceived by the teachers as a long-term learning process. It would seem very desirable for HoEs to make every effort to ensure that the curriculum offered in English was suited to all abilities (since it is a core subject) and, as far as possible, appealed equally to both boys and girls. Departmental meetings need to be held regularly to share good practice as well as to moderate coursework.

The English department usually takes a lead on implementing literacy strategies. As English has traditionally been taught by some part-time staff, perhaps the professional development needs of these teachers should be addressed in order that they might be used as effectively as possible.

Heads of Mathematics

A total of six themes emerged from an analysis of the data and these are described in Table 8.3. As the content of the Mathematics curriculum is prescribed in some detail, HoMs can concentrate their efforts on using departmental meetings to plan schemes of work which are more closely tied to the needs of individual pupils. As it is a core, high-status subject, a great deal of attention has to be paid to monitoring the quality of teaching and learning in a performance-management culture in a similar fashion to that in English.

HoMs would have to spend some of their time liaising with colleagues in primary schools to ensure as much continuity between KS2 and KS3 as possible. This may help to address the issue of the perceived lack of mathematical knowledge on the part of some pupils on entry to the secondary school. There may be some professional development issues regarding the teaching of attainment target 1 (called 'Using and Applying Mathematics' in both England and Wales), which involves the application of Mathematics to practical tasks and real-life problems. These issues may apply to this attainment target if it is taught by non-specialists.

Heads of Science

A total of six themes emerged from an analysis of the data obtained in Phases 1 and 2. These are shown in Table 8.4. In common with English and Mathematics, Science enjoys high status as a core subject. As a consequence of this situation, HoSs need to have a clear idea of how they can draw up suitable schemes of work to help pupils achieve high standards in the GCSE examinations as well as motivating both boys and girls to take Science beyond the age of 16. This would have to be done in a number of departmental meetings over time.

In a performance-dominated culture based on outcomes, the Science staff are clearly under pressure to encourage pupils to achieve the highest possible marks for their investigation work. This may mean that HoSs need to use school-based INSET to address these issues. The HoSs also have to monitor the quality of teaching and learning carefully in a diagnostic way, in order to raise standards across the Science department. All Science teachers need to have a good understanding of how the scientific knowledge of the pupils can become more sophisticated, which may mean that time is used in departmental meetings to agree ways in which activities are planned which help to develop the pupils' understanding and not merely repeat work that has already been covered.

Heads of Technology

A total of six themes emerged from an analysis of the data and these are shown in Table 8.5. Several other useful comments were made by Heads of Technology. One commented upon the differences between girls and boys in the ways they approach Technology:

> I find that the boys tend to be much more interested in doing the practical work and want to spend as little time as possible in designing and the girls will tend to want to put more work into the design folder and are not quite so interested in doing the practical work.

As far as unique methods of teaching are concerned, two different ideas were suggested by HoTs. Firstly, if the Technology staff teach in adjoining rooms, then it is possible to do some team teaching. This leads to a sharing of expertise which can be very beneficial to the pupils. Secondly, one HoT claimed that Technology as a subject can make more demands on pupils compared to other subjects. For example:

Table 8.4 The distinctive features of Science as a subject and their implications for teaching and learning

Subject: Science Distinctive features	Further comments and implications for teaching and learning
A core subject within the National Curriculum	According to some of the HoSs, if all the Sciences were to be covered properly, it would need 30 per cent of available curriculum time for the higher-ability students to cover the syllabus (Phase 1). In Phase 2, most of the HoSs interviewed agreed that Science enjoyed high status within the National Curriculum as a core subject. One HoS felt that the distinctive nature of Science was to 'promote the development of careful observation', which would then 'teach pupils that scientists make models to explain phenomena'.
Science perceived to be a practically based subject	Most of the HoSs considered that Science was a practically based, investigative subject which provides enjoyment and motivation for pupils (Phase 1). However, many of the respondents pointed to specific negative inhibitors of the investigational approach needed to meet the first attainment target. The comments made by HoSs included: 'pupils find higher levels difficult to achieve; there is considerable work involved in teaching this aspect across 3 subject areas; the method of assessment is not workable at KS3; pupils need to be taught the rules and procedures of this type of whole investigative work before embarking on complete Sc.1s'.
The prescriptive content-based nature of the Science curriculum	Some of the HoSs felt that there was too much prescription of the Science curriculum content (Phase 1). Some of them expressed a number of concerns about the effects on teaching and learning; typical comments included: 'does little to enhance prospects of pupils carrying on with Science at A level; teaching now too prescriptive; more traditional teaching methods used to cover the content'.

Table 8.4 *(continued)*

Appeal of Science to both boys and girls	Most of the HoSs claimed that they had tried to ensure the subject appealed equally to both boys and girls (Phase 2). This theme has important pedagogical implications. One HoS felt that the gender balance among the Science staff (i.e. two female and three male teachers) did help to promote the notion of equality in Science. Another HoS noted that: 'the boys have a more positive attitude towards Science than girls, yet girls seem to do better in Science than boys. We do try, for example with our Science 1 investigations, to place them in context where they will be equally accessible to boys and girls.'
Reliance on cumulative knowledge	There was general agreement among the HoSs interviewed in Phase 2 that Science relied on cumulative knowledge, as it is content-based and, according to one HoS: 'without certain groundings, then other things don't follow on; i.e. it has to be organised in a hierarchical sense.'
The everyday relevance of science as a subject	The notion that Science was considered to have everyday relevance and to be vital for so many careers, was noted by some HoSs (Phase 1). The subject was seen as having a variety of cross-curricular links; for example, to number and language skills, energy and the environment, human biology and industry.

Table 8.5 The distinctive features of Technology as a subject and their implications for teaching and learning

Subject: Technology Distinctive features	Further comments and implications for teaching and learning
Technology as a design and make activity	Many of the HoTs considered that Technology was essentially a design and make activity, involving conception of an idea through to practical outcome (Phase 1). Technology was seen as a practical subject, involving hands-on learning using practical skills with a wide range of materials. One HoD commented that: 'it was possible to set a real context where pupils can learn through doing and realise their own ideas'.
Technology encourages the development of problem-solving skills	Some of the HoTs in Phase 1 claimed that Technology was the only subject that asks pupils to think and engage in open-ended problem-solving. The comments made by HoTs included: 'it is difficult to teach pupils to think and solve problems. It is done progressively from Years 7 to 13 and requires a very structured approach' and 'problem solving is more difficult for the lower end of ability range who would prefer to do more practical elements'.
Technology encourages the use of active learning techniques	Some of the HoTs noted that pupils worked both in teams and independently in an informal environment (Phase 1). These HoTs considered that Technology staff need to draw out ideas from pupils rather than spoon-feeding them. The pedagogical implications were that certain foundation skills needed to be taught in Key Stage 3 to ensure more complex tasks could be carried out. According to one HoT: 'flexible approaches are used, which can make it difficult to organise classroom activities when pupils are pursuing different topics at different levels'.

Table 8.5 (*continued*)

Enjoyable subject giving pupils a sense of achievement	For some of the HoTs an important subject paradigm was that Technology as a subject was fun and enjoyable as it encouraged self-discipline, inquiry, ingenuity and gave pupils a sense of achievement (Phase 1).
Lack of status within the National Curriculum	In Phase 2, several HoTs interviewed felt that the subject lacked credibility with Headteachers, compared to other core subjects like English and Mathematics. They considered that Technology had a poor image; for example, one HoT described it as a 'therapy' subject. However, another HoT felt that the subject was distinctive due to its breadth: 'We've got ICT; control technology including electronics; working with the different resistant materials ...'
The need for specialist facilities	There was general agreement among the HoTs interviewed as to the need for specialist facilities. It was acknowledged that it was an expensive subject, in terms of facilities and resources. Loss of workspace can put pressure on teachers to provide pupils with adequate working facilities. According to one HoT: 'we have lost specialist rooms to other subjects and now we are down basically to 3 rooms. One of those we will have to develop away from the original concept of the room which was a metalworking area. ... It'll be more of a multipurpose design room particularly geared up to teaching Electronics.'

it's not teacher centred in most instances any more; it's totally pupil centred with guidance very often as and when the need arises. Success in the subject depends a great deal on the pupil and on the ability of the teacher to motivate the pupil to go and do work on their own.

As far as organizing the subject is concerned, the HoTs need to manage their available facilities carefully and make the most effective use of the skills which the Technology teachers have. They also need to be able to be astute in their management of the external relationships with the Headteacher, SMT, governors and the wider community as Technology is not a core subject and therefore lacks the status of core subjects. However, a school with a thriving Technology department can market itself to parents as offering a richly enhanced curriculum.

Summary

The evidence presented here indicates that the reality of managing a subject largely depends on the nature of the subject itself. There may be a set of common expectations which the SMT have of all HoDs but the actual experience is heavily contextualized within each subject area.

There were some similarities in the comments made by HoDs about subject distinctiveness. Heads of English, Mathematics and Science all referred to their areas of the curriculum as being core subjects, prone to the twin pressures of high status and public accountability. In contrast to Heads of Technology and English, Heads of Mathematics and Science generally felt that their subjects were dominated by prescribed content and a reliance on cumulative knowledge. Heads of Science and Technology generally considered their subjects to be practically based, requiring specialist workshops or laboratory facilities.

Heads of Science and Technology commented more on the different responses of boys and girls to their subjects, whereas Heads of Mathematics and English confined their comments to the underachievement of boys, as well as the steps being taken to remedy the gender-based imbalance of performance. None of the HoDs questioned felt that timetabling restrictions were distinctive characteristics of their subject. Similarly, none of the subject HoDs made any claim to use unique methods of teaching. Several Heads of Technology tried to claim certain key features for their subject but these could easily be refuted. The 'unitary' nature of Mathematics departments was more evident than that of English departments. Heads of English expressed a wider range of views on subject distinctiveness compared to Heads of Mathematics, even allowing for a larger number of Heads of English participating in Phase 1 of the research.

It was somewhat more surprising to find that there were relatively few examples of characteristics described by HoDs as distinctive which could be considered as being *unique* to a particular subject. Only five emerged from a detailed analysis of the data.

- For Heads of English, the emphasis on the acquisition of skills such as speaking, reading and writing meant that the subject made a very important contribution to the development of pupils' abilities in literacy and oracy, which are used across the whole curriculum. This was in marked contrast to the views of Heads of Mathematics where the cross-curricular nature of numeracy skills elicited comment from only a small number of Heads of Mathematics.

- Heads of Mathematics placed great emphasis on logical thinking and encouraging pupils to work in a step-by-step fashion.

- For some of the Heads of Technology, it was the only subject which challenged the pupils to engage in open-ended problem-solving activities. A small number of Heads of Mathematics also considered that problem-solving was an important ability for pupils to develop but in contrast to Technology, the problem-solving activity would not necessarily lead to an end product.

- For Heads of Technology, their subject lacked the status which English, Mathematics and Science enjoyed as core subjects within the National Curriculum.

- Heads of Science felt that their subject placed considerable emphasis on cumulative knowledge, which was also true to some extent for Heads of Mathematics.

Discussion points and practical activities

1. Identify the distinctive features of the subject you teach/ have responsibility for, and list them in Table 8.6 for the categories shown:

Table 8.6   The distinctive features of my subject

Category	Distinctive features
Status within the National Curriculum	
Need for special facilities	
Reliance on cumulative knowledge	
The extent to which the subject appeals to both male and female pupils	
Unique methods of teaching employed in your subject	

2. What is the balance in your subject between the acquisition of skills and the understanding of factual information?
3. How does the working context in your subject differ from other subject areas in the school?
4. To what extent do you think that the Busher and Harris (2000) classification of subject departments (see Table 8.1) is a useful typology? Where does your subject 'fit' within this classification?
5. If you are a Head of Design and Technology/Mathematics/Science/English, to what extent do you agree or disagree with the findings from the research discussed in this chapter?

Further reading

Busher, H. and Harris, A. (2000) *Subject Leadership and School Improvement* London: Paul Chapman.

Gold, A. (1998) *Head of Department: Principles in Practice*, London: Cassell.

Siskin, L. S. (1994) *Realms of Knowledge: Academic Departments in Secondary Schools*, London: Falmer Press.

Siskin, L. S. and Little, J. W. (1995) *The Subjects in Question: Departmental Organisation and the High School*, New York: Teachers' College Press.

9 Learning from experience

Introduction

Prior to the introduction of the National Curriculum in 1988, it was possible for the role of the HoD to be enacted in an almost entirely administrative manner. However, the pace of change in terms of educational policy has been such that HoDs working purely in this way would not be able to discharge all their delegated responsibilities effectively.

HoDs have had to accept responsibility for additional tasks such as the induction of new staff, dealing with frequent changes to the National Curriculum, initiatives concerning key skills and monitoring staff performance. Therefore, the demanding nature of subject leadership and the high expectations placed upon HoDs, means that the ad hoc training, which many existing HoDs have received in the past, will simply not be good enough if future subject leaders are to lead their departments effectively.

All of this raises a number of very interesting questions. How can aspiring HoDs best be prepared to undertake the job? What sort of support do HoDs currently in post need to do their job more effectively? What sort of training is needed for both aspiring and current post holders? To what extent do HoDs perceive themselves as being proactive in the professional development of departmental staff? The argument presented in the rest of this chapter tries to address these questions and is based on the assumption that subject leaders are first and foremost socialized into their role as a result of direct contact with those either doing the job when they are in post or with those doing the job before they were appointed to the position. The notion that an individual can be trained to carry out the job effectively by attending off-site management-based INSET courses is firmly rejected by the author.

The latter part of this chapter will present some research evidence from interviews conducted among a sample of HoDs in Phase 2 of the research to investigate how they have been able to lead and manage their departments successfully and to find out the extent to which they saw themselves as being proactive in the professional development of their colleagues.

Background

Newly appointed SLs

Once appointed, the new subject leader has to establish their own professional credibility with the rest of their colleagues and become, in the terminology used by Brown and Rutherford (1998), the 'leading departmental professional'. In a small-scale study of under-performing departments Harris (1998) noted that:

> the HoD, in most cases, was not someone who was respected by those within the department as an expert practitioner. In fact, there was frequent criticism of the teaching approaches employed by the HoD by departmental members. The study revealed that not one of the teachers in any of the less effective departments had taught with nor been invited to teach with another member of the department ... such a clear absence of collegiality ... was considered to be a major contributory factor to poor performance. (p. 273)

Thus, professional credibility with one's colleagues becomes an essential feature of effective leadership and management, as well as being a necessary prerequisite for the aspiring SL in their metamorphosis from 'follower' (i.e. being a member of a departmental team) to 'subject leader'. Learning to be an effective subject leader is predominantly an evolutionary on-the-job training process, which is by and large, dependent on the potential leader being allowed to take charge of or be responsible for particular aspects of departmental work; for example, being Key Stage 3 curriculum coordinator. This could involve lengthy discussions with other staff about the content of the scheme of work and the possible revision of the assessment procedures, thus providing the opportunity for that individual to develop and demonstrate key leadership skills.

Training and preparation for the role of subject leader
Traditionally HoDs are appointed on the basis of proven classroom competence and the acquisition of sufficient experience of teaching. For example, of the 204 curriculum managers questioned in my survey of HoDs working in Welsh secondary schools, the average length of teaching experience was twenty-one years in Phase 1. Only twenty (10 per cent) had been appointed to lead a major department (i.e. English, Mathematics, Modern Languages, Science) in a medium to large-sized secondary school with less than twelve years' teaching experience.

One possibly fruitful line of enquiry might be to consider the influence of previous HoDs, with whom that individual has worked in previous schools or as a departmental member of staff in their present school. Marland comments on the results of on-the-job training (or the lack of it!) for aspiring HoDs, when it comes to interviewing prospective Heads of department.

> You realize from the candidate's answers and even their questions, that you are really interviewing the distant head of department of the candidate. He/she is not present but his/her influence is. (Marland and Hill, 1981, p. 46)

Marland does not really speculate as to the nature of this influence. However, he goes on to highlight the damaging effect of working under a HoD who has failed to take responsibility for the professional development of the departmental staff:

> Sometimes it is impossible to see individuals as a potential head of department because they have worked in a team with such a poor head of department that they do not really know what the title means. (p. 46)

Another possibility might be to examine the arrangements for in-post training and ask SLs to evaluate its effectiveness. When discussing the preparation for the role of subject leader, Glover *et al.* (1998) note that:

> when evaluating the training offered to middle managers, it has become clear that the most common experience has been as a member of school-based 'hit and miss management' courses, offered as a basis for understanding increased responsibilities

within the school. Interviewees contend that although they are better than nothing, they are of limited value to those seeking career progression. (p. 289)

Their research found that learning-on-the-job was more valued from a developmental perspective. They argue that a large number of middle managers have:

grown into their roles, but such ad hoc arrangements may not be adequate for the changing demands being placed upon subject leaders . . . these people need to have structured opportunities to reflect upon their role. (p. 290)

Different perspectives on learning from experience

The ideas used in this chapter to analyse the evidence refer to three different perspectives on the acquisition of professional knowledge about subject leadership.

First, there is the notion of the reflective practitioner. Schon (1983) advocated this idea in the context of the individual members of staff developing knowledge, understanding, skills and attitudes, on the basis of on-the-job learning experience. This is essentially a potent mixture of reflection-on-action and reflection-in-action. Reflection-in-action is an underdeveloped area of research but could involve asking SLs to keep a diary as they engage in a piece of action research in their own working context. Reflection-on-action is more useful in this context as being relevant to the comments made by HoDs when they reflect back over their work in the department, from the time of their appointment.

Secondly, there are a set of ideas about the ways in which professionals learn when they are almost unaware of the process, referred to as implicit learning.

Eraut (1994) argued that: 'much of the learning about management is unplanned, subconscious and rather haphazard' (p. 82). This implies that over-reliance on past experience could lead to uncritical acceptance of observable behaviour without necessarily subjecting those observations to any kind of critical reflection and analysis. Therefore, he argues that an important aim for management courses might be to 'provide an opportunity to reorganise one's experiential knowledge and bring it under greater critical control' (p. 82).

Eraut acknowledged that much of the experiential knowledge about management is rarely reflected upon by managers and therefore is almost 'unknown' to them. This kind of learning is implicit which may be understood, according to Reber (1993), as: 'the acquisition of knowledge that takes place largely independently of conscious attempts to learn and largely in the absence of explicit knowledge about what was acquired' (p. 5).

It may be argued that tacit knowledge about the role of the HoD is acquired very early on in a teacher's career, observing how teachers relate to each other at close quarters.

The third set of ideas used here are concerned with the ways in which teachers are socialized into their role. Leithwood *at al.* (1994) define socialization as:

encompassing those processes by which an individual selectively acquires the knowledge, skills and dispositions needed to perform effectively the role of school leader. Such processes may range from carefully planned formal education programmes, through less formal but still planned (e.g. working with a mentor) to informal usually unplanned on-the-job leadership experiences. (p. 148)

Although their work was concerned with the socialization of headteachers, the findings from their research which may relate most directly to HoDs include:

most practising school-leaders experience a moderately helpful pattern of socialisation [p. 157]; on-the-job leadership experiences and having broadly based school experiences are seen as being very helpful activities; however, depending on their specific form, they can also be of little use [p. 162]; formal preparation programmes for aspiring and practising administrators appear to vary widely in their perceived value. They are capable of being very helpful or extremely unhelpful depending on their quality. (p. 162)

The socialization of school leaders can take two distinct forms: *professional socialization* of the individual school leader, which, according to Hart and Weindling (1996), when writing about school leaders from a headteacher's perspective, can be defined as:

the process through which a person acquires the habits, beliefs
and knowledge common to and accepted by members of a profession. (p. 314)

and *organizational socialization*, which they similarly define as:

the process through which a person acquires the habits, beliefs
and knowledge shared by the members of a particular organisation. (p. 314)

Organizational socialization is strongly related to the context in
which individual HoDs are actually working. Departments will
vary in composition and experience from school to school. Turner
and Bolam (1998) referred to them as situational factors.

The various components which comprise professional socialization can include, according to Hart and Weindling (ibid.):

management courses for certification (mandatory and voluntary);
first-hand experiences of leadership and management tasks; modelling and social learning (learning by observing both good and
bad models) help form a notion of what is good and bad leadership;
and deliberate mentoring by some existing school leaders who see
importance in their role in preparing future leaders. (p. 315)

The emphasis in terms of the organizational socialization of HoDs
is quite specific to the school in which they are working. In reality, it
means attempting to make sense of the prevailing culture and values
within the narrow confines of a subject department. The newly
appointed HoD may, for example, be one of the younger members
of the department, yet have responsibility for the work of several
staff who have actually been teaching for a considerably longer
period and may be opposed to any changes which the HoD would
think to be worthwhile. It may be argued that there is clear evidence
that all new leaders go through a process of sense-making to deal
with the differences between their expectations prior to appointment, which may well have been formulated in another school
while working with other HoDs, and their actual in-school experiences while working as an HoD.

How did subject leaders learn about the role?

In Phase 2 of my work, 36 HoDs interviewed answered questions about why they behaved as an HoD in the ways that they did and indicated the sources of their ideas about being an HoD.

The evidence collected as part of Phase 2 of the research is presented here in two major sections. The first deals with self-learning about being a subject leader and the second is concerned with the views of SLs about being proactive in the development of their departmental colleagues.

Self-directed learning

The reflective practitioner

Eight (23 per cent) of the HoDs interviewed were able to provide illustrations of how their whole approach to the management of their department altered in the light of their initial experiences on taking up the post. Here they reflect on the lessons learned through hands-on experience. Two examples are included here. The first illustrates the importance of changing one's management style to suit the context of working with fellow professionals. The perceived failure of using an autocratic style resulting in a shift of emphasis towards a democratic, participative approach is clearly spelt out.

> I knew when I was appointed how I wanted to run a department and had to modify that with experience. I started off very dictatorial, very high-handed and realized very quickly that I was offending very experienced people, so certainly I had to learn along the way a lot of people management skills that I didn't have before ... and how did I gain those? By observing other people. I did one or two jaunts out of school and ... learnt that the best way to have success is to make sure that everyone feels that they have ownership. I think that this ownership thing is quite important so my management style is firmly democratic. (Head of English)

The second example refers to learning the art of delegation.

> I think I have learned a lot on the job. There were a lot of things I thought I knew but on reflection I realize now that I had no

idea about. If you take something like delegation. ... The art of delegation is a very complex one and I think that you have to understand what delegation is and what the purpose of delegation is and to whom one can delegate and why and all that sort of thing. If you haven't got that right, then you can spread absolute mayhem all over the place and cause all sorts of ill feeling. (Head of English)

Implicit knowledge about a subject leader

A few of the HoDs found it quite difficult to articulate why they behaved and acted in the ways that they did. This was not surprising in the light of Reber's (1993) notion of implicit learning. For example, one HoD was quite unable to articulate clearly how she managed the department, which can be clearly seen in the following dialogue:

HoD: 'I don't know. Hands-on, I don't know, by perhaps thinking this is what I need for me, and you know, sharing with other people, is this what you mean? I started in the days when there weren't things like schemes of work; the only syllabus was what came from the WJEC' (the local examinations board – The Welsh Joint Examinations Committee)

Interviewer: 'That's right.'

HoD: 'What I needed thinking about as I got more confident in my teaching was perhaps what other people would want. I've always been in a position, mind, where I've always taught with people who've had a lot of experience anyhow. We haven't had any newcomers into the department so I don't know how they'd feel if they. ... I mean we've had some but I think they, you know. ... *I think that's where my vision's come from because of what happened to me perhaps when I was a young teacher.*' (my emphasis)

The conversation with the researcher reflected the difficulties she encountered when trying to unpick the nature of her own implicit learning. At the end, she relates back to her own early formative experiences as a teacher, to explain her own approach to subject leadership.

Socialization

The main idea which can be applied to this section is that of professional socialization, since most of the HoDs had been appointed to their posts, having worked in other schools. What follows are examples of what the process of working with other HoDs means in practice.

The positive benefits

Twenty of the HoDs (56 per cent) interviewed, referred to the lessons learned from working closely with previous HoDs who acted as positive role models. The following examples attempt to unpick some of the benefits. In the first one, the emphasis here is being supportive and providing subject teaching expertise.

> Where I have worked with good Heads of Department, they have been incredibly supportive. They've gone out of their way, (where they wanted change), to make it easy for you to do. They've been friendly and they've always been able to say 'please and thank you' and 'well done'. When things weren't to their satisfaction, they always seemed to manage to be able to tell you in such a way that you didn't quite get your back up. They tended to be, as well, people that were really on top of what they were doing subject-wise, curriculum-wise. (Head of Science)

The second example demonstrates an appreciation of the participative approach to decision-making within the departmental team and the part played by democracy in the sharing out of classes and resources.

> I've always been extremely fortunate to work under Heads of Department who have been kindly, supportive, very professional and democratic in terms as far as they were able, of sharing out the goodies, sharing out the range of classes, being open handed, being even handed in the way that they would give you opportunities (such as they were) for staff development and things like that. ... It was very much a team effort, very much a team building effort and that influenced me greatly. The other Head of Department I went on to work under in the second school again [was] very much involved and interested in his staff, in their development, in supporting them and in the work,

interested in literature and poetry as well as interested in teaching.
(Head of English)

Being a negative influence (i.e. learning what not to do!)
Seventeen of the HoDs (47 per cent) interviewed talked about curriculum managers, with whom they had previously worked, who
exhibited poor leadership skills. The first example demonstrates
clearly how a lack of involvement and being undervalued led to
this former member of a Science department feeling very isolated.

You weren't informed; you didn't know what was going on; you
didn't feel appreciated. You weren't encouraged to be able to do
something however small that allowed you to feel a part of the
department and . . . they tended to be very distant and have very
little to do with you. (Head of Science)

The second example provides some very interesting negative role
models, again shaping what this HoD would *not* want to be like:

Well they've shaped the way I work as a head of department, not
in the way that you would expect in that they haven't been role
models. It's been a case of how not to do it to be quite frank, and
in that sense I suppose they've taught me a lot. I worked really
under two other heads of English, the first I didn't know. As a pro-
bationer I was only acknowledged by her once which was when
she came into my classroom to observe me. She gave me such rigid
schemes of work even down to page numbers of what I was to do,
which I ignored because they were totally unsuitable anyway and
since it wasn't monitored you could do what you liked. So that
was a complete disaster; I felt alienated in the department.

My other head of department, although in fact I thought he
was extremely lazy and I was his second and really felt the brunt
of the work, nonetheless I did learn some things from him. These
were to do with some elements of good practice, of being creative
and of delegating and using people's strengths. So in fairness I
have to say I learned those from him.

What both my heads of department lacked was a real commitment to education and any vision about what it was they were
trying to achieve and those are things that I always felt very
strongly about. That's why I came into teaching. So sadly, they

didn't really shape my own vision of what a head of department should be. (Head of English)

It should be noted that a small minority (i.e. three – nine per cent – of the HoDs interviewed) rejected any notion of learning from previous HoDs, with whom they had worked. In the example included below, the HoD indicates that his way of managing derives from the way he would wish to be treated as a fellow professional. Using Schon's (1983) ideas, it might be argued that this HoD has constructed his knowledge of the role of the HoD, on the basis of reflection-on-past-action.

> No I'm certainly not imitating anybody. I've never been on a course or in-service training to help to be a good Head of Department, so it's basically a 'gut feeling' or how I wish my Head of Department will behave towards me. If you've been a junior teacher for quite a long period of time, you begin to appreciate what it's like. I think you colour the way you run the department by looking back at how you felt you would like to be treated. (Head of Technology)

Other evidence: attending management training courses
Only seven (19 per cent) of the HoDs interviewed mentioned that they had attended any form of management training course. Opinion was divided among the respondents, as to the value of these courses. Eraut's (1994) ideas about the value of such courses for headteachers, is similarly reflected in the comments made by HoDs below.

The positive benefits
Four HoDs discussed the potential benefits of attending a management course. The following example illustrates the benefits of talking with other teachers, or even better, HoDs from the same subject area.

> Apart from learning by making mistakes, the other way that I learn is by meeting other teachers in the authority and talking to them. When you go on a course, you talk to other people and you pick up things but the most important thing of all is that every year, for the last 12 years, we've had a Management course run by the local Authority. It lasts for three days ... we've been to all different places ... we would have people coming in and

talking to us. We would have exercises to do, we would have seminars and you'd talk and this is where you pick up things but it's experience really. (Head of Technology)

No real benefits gained
Three of the HoDs made reference to the lack of any real benefit of attending management courses. The following example shows that unrealistic expectations of such courses affect the attitudes of those attending them.

> I've been on management courses and OK, I've picked up some ideas but I haven't found that I've been on a management course that has significantly changed my approach. Maybe I'm expecting a lot of management courses; maybe you should only go expecting to pick up one or two small points I don't know, but I think I've just arrived at them through trial and error and what seems to work. (Head of Science)

Involvement in the professional development of departmental colleagues

Being a successful subject leader would include adopting a proactive attitude to the training and professional development of departmental staff. This can be achieved by alerting and encouraging staff to attend relevant INSET courses as well as organizing school-based INSET; using departmental meetings to share good practice; involvement in the performance-management cycle; and helping trainee and/or very inexperienced staff.

Use of externally arranged INSET
Twenty (56 per cent) of the interviewees considered that off-site INSET did not play a significant part in the professional development of their colleagues, due in no small part to the quality of the courses on offer. The prevailing opinion appeared to be that the LEA was not providing courses which met the needs of staff. This view was expressed quite forcibly by one Head of English who stated that:

> I don't encourage individuals to attend off-site INSET because I do not think it's good enough and I don't think it is tailored

for individual needs in the way, as a Head of Department, you can tailor it. ·

However, 16 (44 per cent) of the HoDs were able to comment positively on the potential benefits of off-site INSET. Most respondents referred to individual courses which had been attended by members of the department (for example, electronics courses for Technology teachers, evaluating up-to-date Mathematics software for use in teaching, exam board meetings to provide information on assessment arrangements) and several HoDs mentioned the benefits gained by staff participating in the teacher-into-industry placement programme. Despite the lack of support for LEA-run INSET courses, there was some enthusiasm expressed for local arrangements made by consortia of schools which, it was felt, met identified needs much more effectively.

The 'cascade' model commonly used by HoDs, was to arrange for the person who attended the INSET to feed back information to the rest of the department.

School-based INSET
These kinds of activities were widely acclaimed (by 26 – 72 per cent – of HoDs) to be very helpful in the professional development of colleagues, although opinion was divided as to the extent to which they were able to focus directly on teaching and learning issues. More often than not, the agenda for the five training days in the school year was dominated by whole-school issues. Nevertheless, individual examples were noted which illustrated innovative approaches to finding time to deal with teaching and learning issues. These included being able to bid for one whole day off timetable (usually in the Summer Term), and organizing workshops every half-term.

A number of HoDs felt there was a great deal to be gained from detailed discussion of the schemes of work. Other topics suggested for school-based work included dealing with the underachievement of boys; discussing suitable teaching strategies when working with less able pupils; organizing various aspects of Mathematics Attainment Target 1; and help with the management of classroom behaviour.

There were one or two reservations expressed about the value of any kind of INSET process in relation to very experienced colleagues who, it was felt, were reluctant to change the whole approach to their teaching. One Head of Mathematics also mentioned the difficulty of providing INSET in Mathematics for non-specialists who were teaching the subject.

Sharing good practice in departmental meetings

Twenty-nine (i.e. 81 per cent) of the HoDs interviewed made reference to the positive effects of sharing both on a formal level and informally on an almost daily basis. Inevitably there were many positive comments made about the usefulness of sharing good practice in the professional development of departmental colleagues. However, most HoDs were of the opinion that this occurred during informal meetings of the department, rather than formal meetings with agendas.

Heads of different subject areas tended to interpret sharing good practice from a subject perspective. For example, one Head of English used meetings to moderate work in oral examinations; another encouraged departmental staff to bring along examples of activities that had worked well. Several Heads of Science felt that sharing good practice included giving specialists in one of the branches of Science the opportunity to demonstrate unfamiliar ideas to other Science teachers. For another Head of Science, this entailed discussing investigations in such a way as to encourage pupils to achieve higher levels.

Several Heads of Mathematics expressed their views about sharing good practice in terms of discussing the schemes of work and evaluating what worked and had not worked so well. As far as Heads of Technology were concerned, the primary focus of informal discussion centred on strategies to improve the quality of projects being undertaken by pupils. However, they also encouraged specialists in one field (e.g. pneumatics) to help others in their teaching.

Performance management

In Phase 2, the focus of discussion was on appraisal. This has now been replaced with a performance management (PM) system. Nevertheless, the comments made about appraisal have some relevance today because the new PM cycle still involves lesson observation and the setting of targets.

Opinion was fairly evenly divided among HoDs in regard to the effectiveness of appraisal in the professional development. Seventeen

(47 per cent) of the HoDs expressed support for appraisal, although their reasons for doing so vary quite widely. Most appreciated the usefulness of setting targets. One Head of Mathematics described his experience of using classroom observation to give less experienced departmental staff ideas about handling less able, unmotivated pupils. One Head of English expressed the view that appraisal gave the opportunity for staff to be frank about their strengths and weaknesses.

Those who expressed a more unfavourable view on appraisal (i.e. 19 or 53 per cent) gave a wide variety of reasons for its ineffectiveness. Among them were experienced teachers not being willing to accept constructive criticism from their HoD; the excessive demands on time to complete the process properly; and a lack of focus on the real issues concerning teaching and learning.

Working with Newly Qualified Teachers (NQTs) and trainee teachers

Sixteen (44 per cent) of the HoDs either had an NQT(or NQTs) in their department or took part in the initial teacher-training process by mentoring students, or both. Those HoDs working with trainees were clearly aware of the need to provide them with feedback from classroom observation, which would obviously contribute towards their professional development. Those working with NQTs engaged in some classroom observation and provided in-school support. One of the most comprehensive examples was provided by a Head of English who had four NQTs in her department and also had responsibility for three trainees.

> Formal lesson observations have been happening very regularly this year and I visit classroom on an appointment basis, mutually agreed. I've seen each one teach three times this year ... team teaching is a strategy that we use at the lower end of the ability range particularly in the upper school as it is a way of targeting pupils and ensuring that focus and discipline is happening.

Summary

This chapter contains some important messages about the ways in which subject leaders need to prepared for their role and how they might participate in the training of departmental staff.

All the HoDs participating in this research experienced some form of professional socialization as junior members of staff. They appeared to use other HoDs as role models to develop their own knowledge and understanding of the role of the HoD. These role models were perceived either in a positive sense (i.e. in terms of participative decision-making, delegating tasks to others in the department) or in a more negative fashion (i.e. I know I do not wish to behave/act in that way towards departmental colleagues, which might cause them to feel undervalued or even worse, to lose self-confidence).

Most of the HoDs interviewed did not comment on aspects of their organizational socialization, despite being appointed to the post from outside the school. This tends to suggest that some of the learning about being an HoD takes place prior to appointment.

The learning about being an HoD, as derived from management courses, was similar to the kinds of learning experienced by head-teachers. They were perceived as being of quite limited use in terms of their direct impact on the work of HoDs to improve teaching and learning in their department, although they did contribute to a better understanding of the HoD role. This finding may have important implications for the training of existing and aspiring HoDs in terms of the use made of externally run management courses and the possibilities of using expert role models in school.

Most HoDs recognized the need to be involved in the training and development process of their colleagues. Some appeared to be far more willing to be proactive (and imaginative) in addressing important departmental teaching and learning issues. Others felt submerged under the weight of whole-school issues or administrative demands and were consequently less effective in this aspect of their work than they would really wish to be. A minority of those HoDs interviewed felt that off-site INSET courses had much to offer. They felt that such courses improved the subject knowledge of colleagues or expanded their knowledge of assessment arrangements.

In general, HoDs were more enthusiastic about the positive benefits to be gained by departmental staff from organizing school-based INSET and sharing good practice in departmental meetings. Opinion was divided as to whether classroom appraisal was effective in developing the abilities of departmental colleagues. Finally, those HoDs who had NQTs or students in initial teacher training were more proactive in their professional development and perceived it as being an important part of their role to undertake classroom observation.

Discussion points and practical activities

1. If you are an aspiring Head of Department, what delegated responsibilities do you currently hold in your own subject? What other areas of responsibility might you take on, to prepare you more thoroughly for the role of HoD?

2. If you are an existing subject leader, discuss with your line manager (or with the Headteacher), the possibility of job shadowing someone with more responsibility than yourself (for example, a Head of Faculty, Key Stage Coordinator, Assistant Deputy Headteacher).

3. If you are an existing Head of Department, arrange an informal meeting with other HoDs to discuss areas of common interest and share good practice (for example, how each HoD deals with classroom behaviour, assessment, SEN pupils, etc).

4. What positive role models as Heads of Department have you encountered in the past? To what extent are you trying to imitate them?

5. What negative role models as Heads of Department have you encountered in the past? To what extent are you trying to avoid being like them?

Further reading

Brundrett, M. and Terrell, I. (eds) (2004) *Learning to Lead in the Secondary School*, London: RoutledgeFalmer.

Gronn, P. (1999) *The Making of Educational Leaders*, London: Cassell.

Polyani, M. (1967) *The Tacit Dimension*, London: Routledge & Kegan Paul.

Wise, C. and Bush, T. (1999) 'From teacher to manager: the role of the academic middle manager in secondary schools', *Educational Research* 41 (2), 183–95.

10 Subject leaders and the management of continuing professional development

Introduction

This chapter begins by providing a definition of professional development and then attempts to place it in a modern context, in relation to performance management and its implications for subject leaders. A variety of models for continuing professional development (CPD) are then outlined, followed by a discussion of the results of research on this issue. It is possible to engage in a number of different CPD activities. Comments are included from SLs who have been interviewed in Phase 3 about their role in professional development, for some of those listed.

Definition of professional development

The current proliferation of terminology can make any discussion of CPD confusing. For example, it can be seen as staff development, in-service training, and teacher development. A working definition of CPD suggested by Bolam and McMahon (2003) will also be adopted in this discussion. It was first proposed by Day (1997):

> Professional development consists of all natural learning experiences and those conscious and planned activities which are intended to be of direct or indirect benefit to the individual, group or school and contribute through these, to the quality of education in the classroom. It is the process by which alone and with others, teachers review, renew and extend their commitment as change agents to the moral purposes of teaching and by which they acquire and develop critically the knowledge skills

and emotional intelligence essential to good professional thinking, planning and practice with children, young people and colleagues through each phase of their teaching lives. (p. 4)

In the current educational context, CPD can be thought of as
being a balance between activities which might satisfy whole-
school needs and those which address the needs of individual staff.
Bradley (1991) categorized four different types of activities, two of
which would satisfy individual needs:

(i)   those which improve teacher's performance in their present
      job, and
(ii) those which enhance their prospects of career development
      (p. 2)

and two which would satisfy the needs of the school:

(iii) those which help the school improve its present performance
      in areas where it feels deficient; for example, through staff
      changes it might find itself lacking expertise in a certain area
      of the curriculum, and
(iv) those which help the school meet future demands (p. 2)

CPD in the context of performance management

Within the PM framework (discussed in Chapter 1), departmental
staff will be observed teaching at least once a year by an appropriate
line manager. This may or may not be the HoD, as one person may
be responsible for the PM of only three or four other staff. In larger
departments, the HoD may not be fully aware of the training needs
of all members of his/her department. Yet in the TTA (1998) document, there is a clear expectation that HoDs will:

lead professional development of subject staff through example
and support, and co-ordinate the provision of high quality professional development by methods such as coaching, drawing on
other sources of expertise as necessary; for example, higher education, LEAs, and subject associations. (p. 12)

In all secondary schools in England and Wales, some aspects of CPD will inevitably become more tightly controlled as PM becomes more embedded within the culture of teaching. A good example of this process is the Key Stage 3 Strategy. Whereas devolved CPD budgets to schools have become smaller in size, there is less flexibility for SMT (and the Staff Development Officer in particular) to meet the needs and aspirations of all the staff. Whole-school action plans often reflect priorities which arise from inspections. Alongside those are departmentally based plans which outline subject-specific priorities which usually reflect key whole-school issues. On the other hand, there is finance available for training in connection with the implementation of the KS3 strategy.

Models of CPD

There are various models which may be applied to CPD processes. Oldroyd and Hall (1991) place an emphasis on *collaborative learning* within the notion of building the reflective practitioner (as advocated by the GTCW, 2002). Activities such as teacher visits, observation, reflection-on-action and job rotation are examples of staff learning from each other. Having obtained funding from the Welsh Assembly, the GTCW have created five different forms of CPD activity (sharing good practice and exchange of ideas; international visits to share good practice; scholarships to focus on a relevant CPD activity; sabbaticals to enable staff to develop transferable skills in a different environment; and funding to support professional networks) (GTCW, 2003).

Joyce and Showers (1988) are keen on the development of *coaching* programmes in school which can either be peer coaching or different forms of mentoring. These sort of approaches involve theory, demonstration, feedback and follow-up support.

Harland and Kinder (1997) focus on the *outcomes* generated by teachers' accounts of the impact on their classroom practice. They suggest a hierarchy consisting of three orders of outcome, where the third order (i.e. acquisition of new information and encouraging new awareness) is least likely to play a significant part in classroom practice, while first-order outcomes (for example, attendance on an INSET activity leading to a fundamental shift in values on the part of the teacher involved) may have a substantial impact on practice.

Cascade models of CPD open up the whole question about the effective dissemination of new knowledge, understanding and skills when a particular member of staff returns from an externally run course to feed back/share good practice with colleagues working in departments. In my view, it is most unlikely that this process is effective in improving standards of teaching and learning.

As far as needs are concerned, individuals vary as much as anything according to which stage in their career they might be in. For example, a trainee teacher would leave a PGCE course with a Career Entry Profile which highlights areas of further development. A teacher in their induction year would also be expected to draw up an action plan to address new areas of professional expertise or to deal with identified weaknesses. Many of these needs might well reflect issues concerning behaviour management, pedagogical strategies or even subject knowledge. On the other hand, those with middle-management responsibilities might well engage in some form of needs analysis which identifies specific areas of leadership and management where the individual needs to gain more experience or acquire new skills (for example, developing team leadership skills).

Rhodes and Beneicke (2003), in the context of poorly performing teachers, suggest coaching and mentoring as ways in which teacher performance might improve. However, their main argument revolves around the development of a framework which clearly identifies the gap between desired and actual performance based on a needs analysis. They go on to argue that generating explicit learning goals for teachers does not go far enough. They note that:

> Managers need to offer support within the work environment which ensures that teachers have the opportunity to use learned knowledge and skills in conjunction with feedback that encourages reflection. (p. 137)

These comments could equally apply to all staff, not just those who are perceived to be underperforming.

CPD and subject leaders

As has already been discussed in Chapter 9, training and preparation for the subject leader position is very limited. Glover *et al.*

(1998) investigated the views of SLs in seven schools regarding their interpretations of the role of a middle manager and their views of their own professional development needs. They suggested that a detailed analysis of the knowledge and competence required for subject leaders is carried out. This could be done by using the TTA (1998) standards as a starting point and an individual subject leader could carry out a self-audit of their capability.

Adey and Jones (1998) identified a wide variety of professional development needs for SLs. The two most popular categories were developing general managerial skills, and knowing more about school budgeting and financial matters, especially in relation to corporate planning at a departmental level. However, some of the respondents identified planning skills, especially prioritizing aims and objectives and the need to plan in the medium to long term within the framework of whole school policy.

More recently, Harris (2001) investigated the impact of training on the work of subject leaders. She found evidence of a growing trend towards school-based training courses being jointly organized by LEA personnel and those working in higher education. For such courses to be effective, they had to contain an action research element as well as stimulating a debate about pedagogy. In addition, it was felt that support from agencies outside the school was very important.

Adey (2000) did not find any conclusive evidence of an increase in the assumption of responsibility for the professional development of team members. In fact, the emphasis appeared to be one of reactive management (i.e. if the examination results are threatened, then subject leader will take action). This was corroborated in the research carried out by Brown *et al.* (2000) where SLs felt that the opportunities for staff development were limited by lack of funding and/or lack of time. However, Bolam and Turner (1999) did find some evidence that subject leaders valued opportunities to organize school-based in-service training on the five annual training days, as it could be tailored to the needs of departmental staff.

Managing the CPD of departmental staff

According to Craft (1996), there are a variety of different ways of learning and account should be taken of the fact that different people prefer to learn in different ways. She lists the following ten methods, all of which can add to an individual's knowledge, understanding and skills base. It is also important to distinguish between the professional development needs of the subject leaders themselves and the CPD needs of their departmental colleagues.

Action research

Interest in action-research models of teacher development has grown in recent time with the possibility that an individual member of staff might be fortunate enough to be allocated a CPD grant or bursary from the General Teaching Council (GTC) (or GTCW in Wales) which might be sufficient to fund some form of small-scale research in school. In April 2001, the General Teaching Council for Wales invited bids from teachers for a variety of CPD funded activities. One of these was a professional development bursary worth up to £500. One example of its use by a Head of Music can be seen, as follows:

> A secondary Head of Music used her bursary to acquire new technologies to ensure that all pupil performances and compositions were recorded in as professional way as possible. She received two days of personal training in a wide range of areas, including using multitrack minidisk recorder, recording live groups and soloists, the use of microphones and relevant software, mixing music, CD-ROM technology and transferring material from CD to MD and tape. ... The fact that the training was work-based, taking place at the school and using its own equipment, made it a bespoke experience. (www.gtcw.org.uk/pdf/cpd p. 16)

The actual research can usually take the form of investigating the introduction of some sort of change over time (for example, a change to the curriculum). It might also be evaluative in the sense that a judgement might be made at a point in time as to whether the change was achieving all the expected outcomes.

Self-directed study

The stimulus for such activity can arise in a number of ways; for example, when an individual member of staff is asked to teach an area of the curriculum which is not familiar to them or a pupil arrives in the school with an unfamiliar form of special educational need. A teacher starting out in their teaching career will have their

Career Entry Profile which contains specific reference to an area or areas of weakness in professional practice which need attention in their first year of teaching.

Using distance-learning materials

This method may be used by individual staff who have enrolled for a higher degree in Education. Another possibility might be that a teacher might be looking to improve their leadership and management skills using on-line materials which will be accessible on the National College of School Leadership website (http://www.ncsl.org.uk/).

Receiving on-the-job coaching, tutoring or mentoring

All forms of initial teacher education and training now use mentoring as a very important feature of teacher development. For practising teachers, training days may well provide the most suitable setting for coaching where new techniques can be demonstrated and practised with help readily available from other staff with more expertise. This is especially relevant to the use of various forms of ICT in subject teaching.

Coaching was most frequently mentioned in connection with the work done with trainee teachers. An example in this context involves staff in the Science department in Central School, visited in Phase 3, acting as coaches/tutors to staff visiting from other nearby schools who wish to find out more about the use of ICT in the context of delivering the Key Stage 3 strategy in Science.

> We are a lead science department here for the strategy as well, as part of the funding for that I'm investing in another two data projectors for the department and possibly if funds for Key Stage 3 will allow it a third one, so that's a big part of it. Certainly I'd rather have two data projectors than one projector and one whiteboard for similar money, I think they're incredibly powerful.

> Interviewer: You said you were a lead department and you've also talked about going out to other schools. Do people come here as well?

> Yes, the idea of that is that people come here to see some aspects of good practice hopefully that we carry out, so over the last year seven in my department, including NQTs, have actually

delivered lessons to teachers from other schools, which is I think is fantastic and shows the strength of teaching within the department and the confidence and the desire for people to progress.

School-based and off-site INSET courses

These are more traditional types of CPD activity. A criticism often levelled at off-site courses is that they fail to take account of an individual's needs. However, the same cannot necessarily be said for school-based INSET, since any training in school can be more targeted and, as Neil and Morgan (2003) point out, there is more chance of follow-up and opportunities to continue to develop expertise. Five training days (usually used for on-site INSET) are set aside each year in secondary schools in England and Wales, for the purposes of professional development. They are normally devoted to whole-school issues; for example bullying, assessment, target setting, monitoring, school development planning, preparing for inspections, etc. In my experience, very little time is allocated for subject leaders to discuss issues, which directly concern teaching and learning. In addition, there are regular departmental meetings, which seek to deal with urgent matters such as deadlines for administration tasks, curriculum development, particularly where schemes of work require rewriting, GCSE coursework moderation or staffing issues.

As part of school-based INSET, some form of lesson observation can be used. This may take the form of an individual member of staff observing the SL using a new pedagogical technique (for example, using ICT in a lesson by combining Powerpoint with the use of Interactive Whiteboard software). Structured classroom observation is commonplace on initial teacher training courses but has been traditionally very rare in normal practice. This may be because the prevailing culture within the profession is still, to some extent, that of professional autonomy, whose ethos is one of trust in the teacher to do the job to the best of his/her ability without interference.

One other reason why teachers, particularly HoDs, have been reluctant to engage in classroom observation is that they fear a backlash in terms of hostility generated by departmental staff, who see the whole exercise as a 'spying mission', and may perceive any suggestion that teaching strategies could be improved or classroom discipline be tightened up, as a threat to their professional competence.

Over-reliance on school-based INSET at the expense of other forms of training is ill-advised.

Another powerful form of CPD can occur when a member of the departmental team is given the opportunity to provide INSET for other members of staff; it need not necessarily be the sole responsibility of the HoD. An example comes from the Head of English at Central School:

> The second in department has led some on the Year 9 exam. Another member of the department has led some INSET on grammar because the teaching of grammar is a big thing now with the framework. There were some people who didn't really feel secure in their own knowledge of grammar and her degree is English language so she's a real expert on it. She led some INSET for all of us on basic grammar.

This can also be especially useful if certain people are very good at incorporating ideas using ICT into their lessons when other staff are not. If the departmental team is large enough, it can then be sub-divided into smaller working groups. Off-site INSET is commonly used for a variety of purposes. An example of this comes from the Head of Business studies at Highway School who describes how performance management has helped to decide whether attendance on an INSET course would be beneficial to a member of the department:

> One member of my department wants to go on a course; they don't care what course it is as long as they go on a course. They haven't been on a course this year; to me that isn't good use of time or money. It might be if that person has got a specific area that they want to develop in assessment for GCSE, then that's what we should target. That's what we should look at for that individual rather than the member of departmental staff just saying: 'I want to go on a business related course'. To actually do that you've got to go back to performance management, identify what training you've done and what training you need to do.

Very often, any member of staff would be expected to 'cascade' back to the rest of the departmental staff. However, one must question the effectiveness of such a mechanism and question whether those participating in the feedback gain any real benefit from such an exercise.

It is sometimes possible for schools in the same geographical area, in the same LEA, to put their budgets together and organize INSET according to local needs. If they belong to the same consortium, then it is possible to organize a consortium INSET day, pool resources and organize the training to meet the needs of all those in a particular subject.

Job-shadowing and rotation

For an inexperienced teacher wishing to learn more about the pastoral work done in the school, job shadowing may take the form of sitting in on meetings with parents organized by a Head of Year. Its principal aim is to provide a form of on-the-job training as well as giving an opportunity for a professional discussion once the meeting has ended. Many Heads of Department generally allocate responsibilities to named members of the department which can be reviewed on an annual basis. Job rotation can provide all members of the department with opportunities for developing new expertise as well as giving them the chance to develop their career profile.

According to the Deputy Headteacher at Central School:

> I personally feel that the best experience you can get is actually shadowing a head of department rather than going on a course, getting a nice lunch. So what we try to do is to say to somebody who wants to be a head of department; they can either shadow somebody here; they can go to a different school, as well as going on the INSET course. I have not got a problem with that, but rather sort of doing something that is more hands-on than just sitting there listening to somebody talking and filling in things on big spreadsheets.

Membership of a working party

An activity such as this can provide a classroom teacher with an opportunity to gain important insights into whole-school issues. It is only recently, with more widespread use of working parties looking at cross-subject issues, and more staff taking part in higher degree courses, that staff have become aware of the possibility of doing in-school research.

Teacher placement

This kind of activity is sometimes available to a more experienced teacher who wishes to learn more about the exercise of management and leadership in a business context. The aim of such an exercise is to learn from best practice in industry and then to try and apply the lessons learned back in school. Teacher placements may also involve a short period of time spent in another school.

Personal reflection

This form of professional development can be useful in specific situations. For example, if the management of pupil behaviour is an issue for an inexperienced teacher, keeping a diary in the form of a personal account of day-to-day events may be useful in discussions with a more experienced senior member of staff which might help that member of staff develop workable coping strategies. One important aspect of CPD might occur when, periodically, the department reviews and evaluates its practice. For example, this might occur when rewriting parts of the scheme of work is planned. Staff can have the chance to express their views about what changes need to be made to improve the quality of teaching and learning. Often examination results or end-of-module test scores can be placed side-by-side with the aims and objectives for subject courses as part of the evaluation, together with pupils' comments about their feelings concerning the courses being offered.

Collaborative learning

For many teachers, the opportunity to share good practice can occur in departmental meetings and other more informal settings such as a lunchtime discussion. For example, the Head of Mathematics at Highway School commented on the team emphasis to school-based INSET:

> A lot of our INSETs we do very much as a team, so that everyone is developing together and looking at new initiatives that are coming in, giving people small responsibilities within that, so that they take things on board. Within the faculty, I get extra

time for monitoring, but I've used that time to relieve people so that they can go and watch other people within the faculty teaching, so we've done a lot of mutual observations within the faculty as well. I think you can write as much as you like down on paper, but there's nothing like going into a classroom and watching someone else teach, picking up ideas.

There are other contexts which are well suited to professional learning. Team teaching and more recently, staff offering learning support to pupils with Special Educational Needs (SEN) provide opportunities for practice to be shared and classroom performance enhanced. An imaginative use of limited funding is given by the Head of Technology in Highway School who described how, using a consortium approach, collaborative learning might occur:

Our relationship within the consortium has changed quite considerably this year because we are developing a new post 16 product design course. It is a good form of professional development because we are working together, everybody has different strengths and different contacts. We obviously have quite a lot of large plant machinery ideal for rapid prototyping which other centres don't have, so it means that they can use our facilities. They've got expertise and links with other companies that we don't have.

Interviewer: Does that mean then that some of the staff here will go to other places to use things, and will other staff come here to use things, or will pupils go between sites?

No, it can be e-mailed across or it can be video-conferenced across.

Interviewer: It's done that way is it?

Well because we're trying to mirror as much as possible industry and client communication. Therefore we do have an e-mail address which is our product design address which other centres will e-mail us, etc. We get to go to other centres but for meetings, not to deliver. We also have courses like the AVC engineering that we run which is part taught here and part taught at another local school.

Dilemmas facing subject leaders

There are two specific dilemmas facing HoDs which very often limit the effectiveness of INSET.

Conflicting priorities

The rapidly changing national scene with the government issuing a constant stream of educational initiatives and policy changes, can make the process of dealing with different priorities very difficult for HoDs, if at the same time, there are other ongoing school based or departmentally based developments to deal with. This can make the job of HoDs far more problematic as they struggle with the implementation of change. Budgetary constraints also limit the number of INSET opportunities which might be available to departmental staff.

Part-time staff

This problem concerns either staff who work full time in the school but only teach a few lessons in the subject area for which the HoD has responsibility, or staff who only work part-time. In the case of those staff who fall into the former category, it is often very difficult for staff who are 'loosely attached' to attend meetings or training days when they consider their loyalties lie in another curriculum subject.

HoDs managing their own CPD

The evidence presented here represents a range of views which are predominantly subject-specific and context-specific. In the first example, the Head of Music discusses how he has tried to meet the conflicting demands of teaching a full timetable in school while attempting to expand the role of music in the community, in consultation with the Headteacher, who is his line manager.

> My professional development is done with meetings directly with the head, mainly because the head is particularly interested in music ... I would flag up with the head particular things that I felt were areas that I needed to address in terms of improving the

quality of my own teaching. For instance one of the issues for me is time and so in my current meeting with the head one of the things I did was to outline all the things I've been doing this year on top of a full teaching timetable with only three periods a week whereas a head of department is supposed to have four. Now I can't keep on doing this and keep on top of my departmental organisation, but also my own personal planning and delivery of my lessons ... one of the big issues for me is trying to find ways in which I can get more time. One of the reasons I was appointed to the post here was we wanted to develop links between the music department and the wider community at large and we wanted to sort of raise the profile within the community as well as within the school, which has meant that I've taken on a lot of initiatives which involved me in giving up a lot of my own time outside of lessons.

Interviewer: I'm assuming you're talking in these terms because this wasn't really going on before. This was an area that he saw as needing to be developed?

It was seen that there were certain things about music here which were very good, but there were certain things that we both agreed we'd like to see if we can raise the profile. So time has become a huge issue for me and it's one that I've wanted to make him particularly aware of.

In this second example a Head of Languages perceives his own professional development as being closely allied to being a curriculum leader. This entails regular contact with the relevant examination board.

I think for me in terms of what's new. I've got to keep abreast of the changes that are happening. I try and attend what the examination boards are offering. I've got to keep abreast of that to pass it on to the staff, so over the last two years really it's been make sure I'm aware of the A level changes, the GCSE changes and clearly now the Key Stage 3 strategy.

Interviewer: So those meetings would be for things like going through issues that came out of last year's paper, but would they also do things like discuss curriculum developments for the future, would they talk about changes to the curriculum?

I've just received actually from AQA a letter from them asking for some constructive feedback on difficulties we've encountered in delivering, the coursework elements of the course. (Highway School)

Summary

Clearly, subject leaders have a great deal of responsibility for being proactive in the area of professional development at the departmental level. They may well find themselves being the line manager of an NQT as a subject mentor. There is a set of expectations which the SMT might have of their HoDs in terms of being a good role model for teaching and learning. This could involve occasionally coaching less experienced departmental staff using a team-teaching approach. The sheer variety of models of CPD (e.g. collaborative learning, action research, etc.) offer the subject leader different ways of improving the pedagogical expertise of staff. Unfortunately, one of the commonest methods used, cascading, is probably the least effective in generating any change in practice.

As far as managing the CPD of staff is concerned, a variety of methods can be used by HoDs. These include coaching, tutoring, mentoring staff as part of on-the-job training; giving departmental staff the opportunity to lead an INSET session on a training day in school; encouraging staff to attend relevant externally run courses which are capable of meetings the needs of individuals; arranging for a less experienced member of staff to job-shadow a post holder of responsibility (e.g. Key Stage 3 coordinator); and strongly encouraging departmental staff to observe each other teach on a regular basis. This last-named method is very useful as a way of sharing good practice.

Finally, the subject leader needs to take every opportunity to develop their own professional skills by, for example, attending examination board meetings or studying for a higher degree in education.

Practical activities

1. Which of the ten methods suggested by Craft (1996) have been most influential in your own professional development as a teacher (and subject leader if applicable) to date, and why?

2. (a) Which of the other methods suggested by Craft would be most likely to provide the best CPD opportunities, both for yourself and for the departmental staff, in your current working environment?

   (b) What forms of appropriate support (both human and material) are you most likely to need when doing this activity/these activities?

3. Log on to the National College for School Leadership website (www.ncsl.org.uk). Click on 'leadership development' and then 'emergent leadership' to find the details of the 'Leading from the Middle' Programme. Find out as much as you can from the website about this programme and then discuss with the Staff Development Officer or the Headteacher of your school, whether it would be worthwhile enrolling on the programme.

4. Reflect on the different models for CPD outlined in this chapter. Using the following scale, note the potential utility of each of these models in Table 10.1 below:

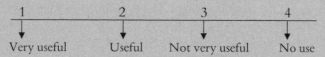

1	2	3	4
Very useful	Useful	Not very useful	No use

Table 10.1   Usefulness of various models of CPD

Models of CPD	Perceived usefulness in CPD terms
Collaborative learning model	
Coaching model	
Cascade model	

5. How could the usefulness of each of these models be further improved?

Further reading

Adey, P. (2004) *The Professional Development of Teachers: Theory and Practice*, London: Kluwer Academic.

Bolam, R. (2003) 'Professional development and professionalism' in Bush, T. and Bell, L. *The Principles and Practice of Educational Management*, London: Paul Chapman.

Burgess, R. G., Connor, J., Galloway, S., Morrison, M. and Newton, M. (1993) *Implementing In-Service Education and Training*, London: Falmer Press.

Clement, M. and Vandenberghe, R. (2003) 'Leading teachers' professional development' in Kydd, L., Anderson, L. and Newton, W. *Leading People and Teams in Education*, London: Paul Chapman.

Earley, P. and Bubb, S. (2004) *Leading and Managing Continuing Professional Development*, London: Paul Chapman.

Mumford, A. (1997) *Management Development: Strategies for Action*, London: Institute of Personnel Development.

Rhodes, C. and Houghton-Hill, S. (2000) 'The linkage of continuing professional development and the classroom experience of pupils: barriers perceived by senior managers in some secondary schools', *Journal of In-Service Education* 26, 423–35.

Tomlinson, H. (1997) *Managing Continuing Professional Development in Schools*, London: Paul Chapman.

11 The management of pupil performance through data collection and analysis

Introduction

Teachers have always collected data on pupil achievement and carried out some form of analysis of examination results. However, since the introduction of National Tests at the end of KS2 and KS3, more top-down 'pressure' has been placed on schools by successive governments to be accountable for the performance of their pupils in public examinations. As a result, Headteachers and governors have increased their expectations of the abilities of HoDs and/or Heads of faculty to monitor standards of pupils' work in the areas of the curriculum for which they are directly responsible.

The views of HoDs and senior managers, collected as part of Phase 3 of this work, are included in this chapter to reflect their views on the management of pupil data.

There is a very wide range of data now available to subject leaders which can be stored on spreadsheets such as Excel and on school information systems such as SIMS, leading to the notion of schools being 'data-rich'. In addition, the Autumn Package (DfES, 2002a) can also assist schools in answering questions as to whether different groups of pupils have performed to expectations in KS3, in the light of their KS2 SAT results, or whether pupils in KS4 have achieved the results in their GCSEs which might have been expected on the basis of their KS3 SAT results.

The main emphasis in the DfES (2002b) document concerned with data management argues strongly that data-rich schools should aim to be information-rich and pass that information on to staff in an easily digestible form. Having the information is one thing; knowing what to do with it is something else.

One of the aims of this chapter is to try and highlight what actions can be taken by the Head of Department and departmental staff in the light of this information. Any member of a school's SMT or SL may be able to access information about pupil attainment across a range of subjects. Individual pupils can have their progress 'tracked' in KS3 and, if their level of progress begins to 'dip' below what might be expected, then remedial action can be taken, to help that pupil realize their potential. This might mean interviewing the pupil about their work; providing a mentor in the form of an older pupil to give advice, support and encouragement.

Joyce et al. (1999) described the wide range of available qualitative and quantitative information about pupil progress (for example, records of disciplinary incidents, attendance rates, truancy rates, literacy and numeracy scores and standardized test results), in support of their hypothesis that 'an information-rich environment will enhance inquiry' (p. 12). By 'inquiry', they mean school improvement and the raising of educational standards. However, the proliferation of this sort of information raises a number of questions. These include investigating whether SLs or Heads of Faculty have access to this wide range of data and if they understand what it means. In addition, there is currently a lack of information about how SLs use data in monitoring the performance of the department and if the use of such data has any direct impact on classroom practice. There is also some evidence from school inspections to suggest that some teachers have not been able to make effective links between pupil performance data and pupil learning objectives (Ofsted 2002).

Types of data available

Rudd and Davies (2002) surveyed secondary school staff working in eight LEAs about their use of performance data. Sixty-eight responses were obtained from secondary heads of departments from 36 schools. When asked about their use of data, the majority (i.e. over 50 per cent) utilized the following *seven* different types:

- *Key Stage SAT results from KS2 and KS3*: raw scores from KS2 National tests would be available to secondary schools in English, Maths and Science. Primary school teacher assessment data in addition to scores from national tests would add to the reliability of the data. Any analysis of KS3 data should take into account that expected progress should equate to moving up one level every two years

- *GCSE results*: these provide a very important benchmark for being able to predict outcomes in KS5

- *Autumn Package*: this contains information which will enable a school to make comparisons with other schools, based on pupil performance in examinations and national tests (DfES, 2002e). Such analyses enable members of SMT and heads of department to determine whether pupils have achieved standards in English, Mathematics and Science which are better or worse than the national average. This information can be used to calculate value-added data (for example, for KS2/KS3 comparisons). Progress charts for pupils with similar attainment scores in KS2 can also be produced showing the percentage of pupils achieving Level 4, Level 5, etc. in KS3 SATs

- *PANDA information*: this is provided to schools in England by Ofsted, prior to an inspection. It contains information about the achievements of pupils in examinations and tests in KS3, KS4 and KS5. It is, in effect, a 'customized' version of the Autumn Package. As well as value-added information, it also contains useful benchmarking comparisons with other schools working in similar contexts

- *CATs scores*: many schools administer Cognitive Ability tests (CATs), developed by the NFER, to pupils early on in Year 7. This information provides a baseline for assessing levels of literacy and numeracy. It can also indicate a basis for making grade predictions at GCSE level and KS3 performance. An alternative system called MIDYIS (Mid-years Information service) also gives an indication of likely outcomes in KS3 SATs tests

- *LEA-produced data*: the LEA will typically collect data from schools and other relevant national sources and then turn this data into a package for a specific school in the form of a data profile (Rudd and Davies, 2002)

- *School-produced data*: if the subject curriculum is modularized, then data from end-of-module tests would be available as the pupils move through from Year 7 onwards

Although not part of the Rudd and Davies (2002) work, it may well be that some useful data might emanate from an inspection report and, in addition, learning styles data which can be useful. The Headteacher of Highway School recognized the value of ensuring that staff had ready access to a comprehensive set of data on all new Year 7 pupils, as can be seen in the following comments:

> The first group that we are going to be working with will be Year 7, so we will make sure that staff have got all the Key Stage 2 results, together with the marks so that they can actually see whether it was a good level 3 or a poor level 4 or whatever. They will also have the CAT scores which give a target score for Key Stage 3. From the very first lesson staff can plan lessons knowing the range of ability and where they're starting from for that group and where they ought to be moving towards.

Uses of data

These can include making predictions about future performance, i.e. setting expectations; setting targets which may include an element of challenge; tracking progress across a key stage; calculating value added, etc. One of the outcomes of research in the field of data analysis is the notion that prior attainment in the form of an average points score (for example at GCSE by using KS3 SAT results) is a good predictor of subsequent pupil performance. This idea is used in calculations of value added across Key Stages 3, 4 and 5.

The government would like HoDs to use data to judge standards of pupil achievement, particularly in KS3. However, the question of interpretation is vital: i.e. what does the evidence reveal? HoDs can see relatively easily whether standards are changing over time on a year-on-year basis. Is it possible to know whether the department is being differentially effective? Are some groups of pupils (e.g. SEN) progressing more quickly than others (e.g. middle-of-the-road pupils)? To what extent are targets being set by teachers for pupils using available data? Do pupils set targets for themselves? The DfES (2002b) document makes it clear that a target should contain some element of challenge. This is in line with current policy initiatives related to school improvement under the banner 'raising standards'.

The appropriate time span over which improvements might be measured is contentious. Progress for many pupils in KS3 is not likely to be linear as many factors can play a part in disrupting learning. For example, family upset, moving house, a change of teacher, illness and absence can all play a part in demotivating pupils. Perhaps the minimum time span should be no less than one year as any shorter period might be severely affected by one of the above factors.

Data can be used to draw up departmental improvement plans. These might include changes to the curriculum; the use of more interactive teaching styles; greater use of formative assessment etc. Other, more qualitative forms of data can also be gathered relatively easily by the HoD. For example, sampling a set of books on a regular basis from different teachers working within the department can help to judge standards and pupil progress. Comparisons can be made between the performance of an individual pupil in different subjects in the same school and between schools in the same subject, where pupils come from very similar socio-economic backgrounds.

Having a comprehensive data set on individual pupils raises the question: What should be done with it? It can be useful in raising questions about the extent to which various teaching methods are used and their impact on pupil learning. A number of examples are now included to illustrate how different heads of department and heads of faculty use data in ten subject contexts.

Uses of data in ten different subject areas

Business Studies

This is a subject which is introduced into the curriculum at the start of KS4. Perhaps the most reliable prior indicator of performance in GCSE is the KS3 mark in Mathematics for teachers of Business Studies. In addition, as the following comments show, it is possible to set homework regularly and mark that work to GCSE standards as a means of monitoring progress:

> I brought in a system whereby the students would do a key assessment, a key homework once a fortnight. That would be marked at GCSE standards and what we'd do is actually monitor their progress and do a predictor for Key Stage 4 and that would

be communicated to them. We'd say 'We think you should be getting a B'; over the two years they can track their progress using this key homework/key assessment and they can see whether they are above their target or below their target or on target. (Head of Business Studies, Woodland School)

English
Having preferred learning style data available to a HoD can help with setting, as this example illustrates:

> In Year 8 we've got their learning styles analysis. We've also got their data on previous assessments, so when we're setting them into Year 9 we're going to use the learning styles data to refine our setting because very often you find in English, you might have 60 kids on Level 5. It can be arbitrary how you put them into groups. (Head of English, Central School)

The same HoE then goes on to reflect on the effectiveness of learning among the different learner types, although she was not able to say whether the department was more effective in teaching pupils with SEN in comparison to middle of the road pupils or more able pupils:

> I think we're effective with kids who are auditory learners. I think we are becoming more effective with visual learners, but, for example, kinaesthetic learners I do not think we're as effective as we could be there at the moment. (Head of English, Central School)

One of the targeted areas within the Key Stage 3 strategy (see Chapter 12) concerns those pupils who have yet to reach level 4 by the time they enter secondary school in Year 7. As part of the strategy, the government has funded the production of the so-called literacy progress units (LPUs) which have then been distributed to schools in England to help pupils who are assessed to be at level 3 to progress to level 4. It is therefore vital that teachers of English in secondary schools obtain more detailed information than merely the raw scores in terms of English at KS2. This is illustrated in the following example:

Even though they got a level 3, a few students have got a level 5 reading score . . . yet low level 3 writing scores, so when the scores have been amalgamated they come to us with a level 3.

Interviewer: In other words what you're saying is English has got the four skills of reading, writing, listening and speaking, but they might be actually very good in one of those, but they've been pulled down to a 3 because they are weaker in one or two of the others.

Yes, and we need to know that because if we don't know, we don't know we are targeting. (Head of English, Woodland School)

Humanities

Working closely with the parents especially in Key Stage 3 may help to offset any early signs of underachievement. This is illustrated in the following example:

We have entry level data in the form of the Key Stage 2 scores and these are extrapolated along with the CATs scores to give some indication of performance at the end of Key Stage 3, and also some indication of likely outcomes at GCSE. The CATs scores are used to inform our planning in terms of pupil groupings and in terms of identifying levels of underachievement and also to form some basis to relay ideas of underachievement to our parents. With pupils we believe are underachieving, I can turn round to a parent and say 'I don't believe your son/daughter is performing to their level and I've got this evidence'. I mean if a child has got a CATs score of 121 and is working at a Level 4 at Key Stage 3, then obviously alarm bells will start ringing and I can do something about it. (Head of Humanities, Highway School)

Mathematics

A large amount of data is available to Heads of Mathematics enabling them to track pupil progress fairly rigorously to check that they are achieving the kinds of results which reflect their ability. The following example illustrates this idea quite well:

We have standardised test scores from Key Stage 2; MIDYIS information; we also do level orientated tests so in Years 7 and 8 they'd have them every term. By the time we get to Year 9 we're doing past SATs papers every half-term so they can see the key areas they need to improve on. We use the MIDYIS data by getting an indication of where that child should be by the end of Key Stage 3. Because of the different skills that are tested we get an idea of where their weaknesses and where their strengths are so you can adjust your teaching accordingly. (Head of Mathematics, Central School)

Another Head of Mathematics described how he put all the data together on one spreadsheet for each year group. All this information was passed on to each member of the department, who could then use it for detecting early signs of underachievement, as well as monitoring pupil progress:

At the beginning of every year I give each member of the faculty their SAT list together with a list of all this data. They can put it straight into their mark books, so they've got what level they're performing at already, so we can actually look at progression as to how a student does over the year. They know that a student has been assessed at say level 5 in Year 7, if they're performing at level 3 or 4 in Year 8, what's going on? Are they just being lazy? Have we not pushed them on? . . . It gives you something to aim for. (Head of Mathematics, Highway School)

Music
Little reliable information is usually passed on to secondary schools from the feeder primary schools in relation to musical ability. In this example, the Head of Music attempts to ascertain the level of musical knowledge and skill early on in Year 7.

In Year 7 we do a little test, which we call a baseline test, which is general musical knowledge test. This gives us some idea of what sort of general knowledge the pupils have got. We find out fairly early on whether pupils have got particular musical talents in that in any projects that we do, certainly in a lot of projects, there is kind of like a skills based element at the start of the project, which leads to an individual assessment. (Head of Music, Central School)

The same Head of Music then commented on how the levels of assessment can become more refined as the pupils move through Key Stage 3. Their achievement can be matched to National Curriculum levels in Music.

> In Year 8 . . . we look at the use of repeating patterns in the skills based element of a project on reggae music. At the start, there's actually a piece of reggae music called 54 46, which has got a repeating bass line and a two chord pattern. So we have a period of about three weeks where part of the lesson time is taken up with the pupils learning how to play initially the bass line, but also using hopefully correct fingerings. Those who manage that bring in the chords part and after three weeks we'll do an individual skills assessment and we've looked at the National Curriculum levels for performing. We've linked these levels to what we think a pupil playing 54 46 will be able to do to get a level 4 at National Curriculum. We then take that level 4 and we break it down into level 4A, 4B and 4C. It may be that a level 4C for instance might be to play the bass line with your left hand using the correct fingering, which would be starting with your thumb and using different fingers for different notes and playing it fluently, so when we do the assessment that would be considered to be sort of slightly above average for Year 8. A rule of thumb is that in Year 8 they ought to be achieving level 4 or above, so somebody who does that and gets a 4C early on in Year 8 is somebody who's potentially got quite a bit of musical talent.

Modern languages
Data can be used in a variety of different ways. In Highway School, pupils are placed in mixed ability groupings in Year 7. Subsequent setting for Year 8 onwards takes place using three pieces of information: the Year 7 examination results, the CAT scores and teacher recommendations. The Head of Modern Languages expressed some reservations about relying too heavily on the results of the Year 7 examination:

> I think, sometimes, the Year 7 examination isn't rigorous enough. They haven't done enough work of rigour for it to be conclusive

in terms of setting, so we have to look at their base data to discover what their potential is.

Physical Education

This subject is similar to Business Studies in that it becomes a formalized academic subject in Key Stage 4. Heads of PE may well use KS3 results in English, Mathematics and Science (taken as an average points score) to provide an indication of likely performance at GCSE. One Head of PE felt that the Science and English scores were the most useful indicators, despite the emphasis placed on the practical side of the subject at GCSE:

> We use basically the Science, Maths and English Key Stage 3 results which give a predictor of performance at GCSE. Primarily I look at the Science and English because there is a scientific background to the PE in terms of the exercise physiology and anatomy areas. Those are our benchmark figures that we set figures for. (Head of PE, Woodland School)

Science

The Head of Science, in the example quoted below, has a range of data including SAT results in KS2, MIDYIS testing in Years 7 and 8, as well as internally generated data from end-of-module tests and end-of-year exams. However, he was keen to see that all departmental staff take into account prior attainment when considering how to improve the standards of teaching and learning.

> We use it [data] for looking at setting at the end of the year. We essentially use our end-of-year exams and internal tests for setting. We'll compare that to other information we've got, such as Key Stage 2 data. Over next year we certainly want to be a little bit more proactive in mentoring and identifying pupils who are falling below what we think they ought to be achieving based on past performance . . . I think we need to try to make staff aware all the time of past performance, so to that end, we'll include this sort of information maybe in a coded form on a register list. So it's there with the teacher in the classroom all the time so they can compare test marks as they happen with the previous information and previous test marks. (Head of Science, Central School)

Technology

The work of a Head of Technology reflects the need to monitor pupil achievement in Key Stages 3, 4 and 5 very carefully. In this subject, there are six specialist areas but they all use the same marking criteria.

> At Key Stage 4 we use CAT scores mainly now and the Autumn Package really to inform our teaching. This data is converted into a target minimum grade, looking at the data we've got. The students are informed of what they can get looking at those tests and then they're given a target grade as well. At Key Stage 3, again that data is available from the CAT tests.

> Interviewer: So you've got all this information, then do you use it in any particular way? Do you use it to look for signs of underachievement?

> Yes, especially at Key Stage 4; we use these target grades, give them to the students and you can see immediately on the record sheet if you're using coursework. There's a sheet that says their current grades for each criteria that we mark against. Then you can see if their minimum target grade is an A and they've got current grades of a D, immediately you can identify that there is an issue. You identify the action that needs to be taken, whether it be just the student just be sorting themselves out with detentions to support it, or whether it's getting parents in, etc. When we get their GCSE mock results in December, students there who have underachieved greatly will be identified. (Head of Technology, Highway School)

Vocational Studies

In Highway School, this faculty includes a range of subjects such as Health and Social Care as well as Business Studies. The Head of Faculty sets target minimum grades for pupils in Key Stage 4, in the following way:

> At Key Stage 4 in the past there have been target minimum grades set for Business Studies based on data. There's been nothing for Health and Social Care in the past, but we this year just started using an average of their Key Stage 3 scores and setting a target minimum grade from that. (Head of Vocational Studies)

Subject leaders and the use of value-added information

It is possible to analyse KS3 results in terms of value added in relation to KS2 performance. One way might be to use the Autumn Package to do this. In the following example, a Head of Science outlines the results of such an analysis and speculates as to the reasons:

> From some of the analysis I've just done with Year 9 SATs it suggests that the top group, Set 1 out of 8, had the highest value added compared to Key Stage 2 SAT results for about just over one and a half levels. It gradually got less and you could draw a reasonably straight line through it. Now is that as a result of the teachers or as a result of the groups? I don't know. I also went to a meeting with other Key Stage 3 co-ordinators and heads of department the other week from other schools and they anecdotally said they'd noticed similar things. I think probably the language of the SATs has a lot to do with that. The lower groups just can't manage the English content of the SATs. There is almost more writing in it than the GCSE papers I think.
>
> (Head of Science, Central School)

The Head of Science at Highway school used the Autumn Package to analyse the progress of groups of pupils across KS2 to KS3, or KS3 to KS4. He was able to carry out comparisons between groups of pupils of different abilities as well as by gender, as can be seen in the following comments:

> Different groups make different amounts of progress but it's not that simple because they are also setted and they are taught by different teachers ... I looked at their CAT scores, which are supposed to be a basic indicator of ability and I put them into ability ranges and then I looked at the end of Key Stage 3 results and compared to those in Key Stage 2. So I looked at the progress they'd made across the Key Stage and compared it to their CAT score. I could then say that the less able students comparatively make better progress than the middle range students ... That's not necessarily the pattern I saw, but I was able to look at the different ability ranges and say whether or not they'd made the same amount of

progress across the Key Stage. I could separate that into boys and girls as well. . . . It was more difficult to decide what to do with the patterns that were identified. We could identify, say, the middle ability boys aren't doing as well as the middle ability girls. What do we do? What do we do with the boys who aren't making as much progress as the girls? What do we do about behaviour?

These questions can be used as a basis of departmental discussions about improving the standards of teaching and learning.

The Head of Mathematics at Highway School also used the Autumn Package to do a set by set analysis to look at progression in terms of value added achieved by specific groups of pupils.

The Head of Vocational Studies at Highway school was able to describe how she calculated value added using baseline data obtained from an average points score from KS3 SATs results. However, she also carried out comparisons between the results obtained in the subjects in her faculty and those gained in other schools, as a benchmarking exercise.

Reliability of data

Questions were raised as to the way in which the National Curriculum level descriptors are mismatched when comparing performance in KS2 and KS3. According to this Head of English:

> it seems that a level 5 by a kid in Year 6 is completely different in quality and all sorts of other ways to a level 5 by a kid in Year 9 and at the moment, this is a national thing by English teachers. There is a lack of progression, really clearly defined progression. (Central School)

A similar point in regard to a lack of progression was made by another Head of English in relation to what might be needed for Level 4 in English in KS2 compared to KS3:

> The issue is that you've got to move students on to more mature and more sophisticated texts, so actually to get a level 4 at Key Stage 2 the text that's used to gain that level 4 for them to demonstrate those skills and their understanding are not the same type of

texts or the same sophistication of texts used in Key Stage 3, so that's the difference. (Head of English, Woodland School)

An associated difficulty arises in a subject like History when Heads of History try to credit their students in terms of National Curriculum levels. The level descriptors in History are written in a skills framework. Any improvements in the pupils' knowledge and understanding of the subject are not recognized. One Head of History has tried to bypass these levelling problems by using a computerized 'tag' which matches the requirements of a set of assessment tasks, as can be seen in this example:

> We've identified in the course of a year certain assessment tasks that we'd like all of our Key Stage 3 students to do. We mark those very thoroughly and give very precise feedback on what they've done well and what they need to improve on. We actually use computerised tags (in the form of a label) that we can stick on, that we've created ourselves to say why this a good piece of work and what to build on. ... If a child writes a Level 3 piece of work the label already says this is a good piece of work because ... ; to get to Level 4 you need to do. ... We made them more precise to our assessment tasks and they are computerised, so we run them off and then cut them up and stick them on the pieces of work. To me that's a much more precise diagnosis of where that child has done very well and what they need to do rather than just a number. (Head of History, Woodland school)

Summary

The increasing degree of sophistication and detail which characterizes data at the present time means that subject leaders can now track the progress of pupils in KS3 and KS4, as well as being able to check that each pupil is achieving marks in examinations which, at the very least, match their expected levels of achievement. Most schools administer some form of baseline testing in Year 7 (e.g. CATs) which can give HoDs a predicted GCSE grade for all pupils in the cohort. The evidence presented from the research done in Phase 3 indicates that HoDs in a variety of subject areas use data in slightly different ways to monitor progress in KS3. HoDs appear to place particular emphasis on latent potential which may not have been fulfilled in KS2. In KS4, targets can be given to pupils in terms of likely GCSE grades in specific subjects.

It is now possible for schools to compare the performance of their pupils in KS3 National Tests for the core subjects with their previous levels of achievement in KS2 and thereby calculate their value-added scores using the Autumn Package. However, the reliability of such information will only improve if the data is collected over a minimum of a three-year period.

Discussion points and practical activities

1. Analyse the most recent set of KS3 National Test results and compare them to the results from KS2. Calculate the value-added scores for the Year 9 cohort using the Autumn Package. Compare and contrast the performance of three broad bands of pupils (top, middle and lower) in KS2 and KS3. Which band of pupils appears to make most progress and explain why that might be? Are there any significant differences between the achievements of boys and girls?

2. To what extent do departmental staff have access to performance data and how well do they understand it and use it?

3. If you are a subject leader in a core subject, use the Autumn Package to decide how well pupils in your subject have done compared to pupils nationally.

4. What strategies are currently in place to help pupils who underperform in KS3? Find out from other HoDs what strategies they use which you also might find useful.

5. To what extent are the targets set for performance in KS3 and KS4 being met at the current time? What intervention strategies might be used to help the underachievers?

Further reading

Blanchard, J. (2002) *Teaching and Targets: Self-Evaluation and School Improvement*, London: Paul Chapman.

Fizgibbon, C. T. (1996) *Monitoring Education: Indicators, Quality and Effectiveness*, London: Cassell.

MacGilchrist, B., Myers, K. and Reed, J. (1997) *The Intelligent School*, London: Paul Chapman.

12 Subject leaders and the management of the Key Stage 3 strategy

Introduction

The National Literacy and Numeracy strategies were put in place in England in 1997 and they were accompanied by targets set by the Secretary of State for Education. The percentage of pupils achieving level 4 or above at the end of KS2 were expected to rise from 57 per cent in literacy and 54 per cent in numeracy in 1996 to 80 per cent and 75 per cent respectively in 2002. In the event, the corresponding literacy levels rose to 75 per cent and numeracy levels rose to 73 per cent. Fullan (2003) cites this as a rare example of how a top-down change can be successful. However, this has not been achieved without some cost. According to Galton *et al.* (2003) one effect of the top-down pressure to achieve results in the KS2 SATs has been a 'narrowing' of the curriculum in Year 6 so that different kinds of intervention can occur. The most popular were practice tests which could be carried out and 'booster' lessons to help pupils with basic literacy and numeracy skills. This was often being done at the expense of lessons in music, art and other extra-curricular work.

It was felt by policy-makers that more needed to be done to sustain the improvements in pupil performance that had occurred in KS2 in KS3, particularly in the transition years of Years 6 and 7. This was because analysis of test data in the latter part of the 1990s indicated that pupil attainment 'dipped' in Year 7. Galton *et al.* (1999) estimated that up to two in every five pupils failed to make the progress that might be expected in Year 7 when they transfer from Year 6 to Year 7. This assertion appears to be based mainly on Ofsted evidence and on the performance in tests taken in Years 6 and 7 in Mathematics, English Language and Reading of a sample of 300 pupils. However, it is worth pointing out that the differences were quite small, i.e. a reduction of three or four marks on a 33-item test for most pupils.

In response to the perceived need for firm action to be taken at government level, the ideas for the Key Stage 3 strategy were formulated, building on some of the successful features of the literacy and numeracy strategies. In England the KS3 strategy has been adopted as a top-priority funded policy initiative. In Wales, this has not been the case mainly because funding for such initiatives is much more limited than in England.

Given this policy background, the main purpose of this chapter is to discuss the involvement of different subjects in the KS3 Strategy and to present the perceptions of subject leaders concerning its implementation.

The Key Stage 3 strategy

There are four interrelated aims for the KS3 Strategy. They are fundamentally targeted on bringing about a change in the culture of teaching:

✓ Expectations: this concerns raising expectations for all pupils based on a policy-driven agenda dictated by central government which desires to see improvements in educational standards to justify increases in the spending on education in recent years.

✓ Progression: this relates to progression in KS3 and between KS2 and 3. One of the side-effects of the attention being paid to progression is to try and promote more discussion between primary and secondary staff in order to improve continuity in curriculum terms.

✓ Engagement: the strategy aims to improve the motivation levels of all pupils by encouraging the use of more active teaching and learning approaches. For example, the use of ICT in lessons has been highlighted in the Science framework (DfES, 2002a). In this document it is claimed that the use of such strategies can enhance individual learning as well as that of the whole class.

✓ Transformation: the use of targeted funding for CPD activities designed to improve teaching and learning. This, it is hoped, would bring about a transformation in the culture of teaching. This means, for example, using a credible and appropriately trained subject leader in a funded 'consultant' role to advise partner schools in the local LEA. He/she can help to disseminate good practice and be readily available to assist other subject leaders.

There are various elements which contribute to the strategy and they complement ideas contained in the QCA schemes of work for KS3. They include the following:

Auditing standards of teaching and learning throughout the Key Stage

This would involve discussion with teachers about the use of different teaching strategies which might be employed in KS3 and monitoring the performance of pupils in tests carried out at appropriate intervals. The use of auditing can be used as a way of identifying any changes that need to be made to the existing repertoire of teaching strategies to raise standards of achievement. If baseline data is available (from CATs' scores for example), then the progress of pupils can be carefully tracked to ensure that pupils are achieving the attainment levels anticipated.

Participating in whole-school initiatives (e.g. in literacy and numeracy)

Recognizing that most subject areas can contribute to raising levels of attainment in basic skills such as literacy, then each subject leader may well be able to lead a departmentally based discussion on ways of improving these skills in normal lessons.

Transition from KS2 to KS3

The KS3 National Strategy Framework document for the teaching of Science (DfES, 2002a) suggests that one way of improving transition may be by providing a summer school for pupils to attend. However, it is likely that a more achievable solution could be through the introduction of transition units which could be studied in Year 6 and then be continued in Year 7 to provide curriculum continuity. In the government's view, it is a matter of concern that some pupils do not achieve a level 4 by the age of 11 years. Thus, part of the strategy involves targeting pupils who enter secondary school with level 3 in English, Mathematics and Science to enable them to achieve level 4 as quickly as possible. In English, this has meant that special units have been designed and introduced to help improve literacy in Year 7. These so-called six literacy progress units aim to target perceived problems with writing skills.

Providing booster support for Year 9 pupils
If the government targets level 5 as being the norm for pupils at the end of KS3, then extra support becomes necessary for pupils achieving a level 4 in Year 9. The responsibility for the implementation of the strategy is devolved to the subject leader in the relevant area of the curriculum. The range of responsibilities is spelt out in some detail in each of the core subjects in KS3. However, a member of the school's SMT would normally be appointed to be the KS3 Strategy Manager. His/her role is mainly focused on ensuring internal consistency across different departments in terms of the implementation of the strategy and on administering the DfES Standards' funding budget delegated to the school.

The involvement of different subject areas

When it was introduced in 2000, the KS3 strategy was specifically aimed at raising standards in the core subjects in England of Science, English and Mathematics. In addition, the key skill of developing ICT capability was also integrated into the KS3 strategy and the framework document for this was published by the DfES in 2002 (DfES, 2002c). Pilot work in some foundation subjects (e.g. Modern and Foreign Languages and Design and Technology) is currently being carried out and will not be considered here.

English
The KS3 framework document (DfEE, 2001a) was the first to be published along with the one for Mathematics and has influenced subsequent thinking about this strategy. It recommended a four-phase lesson structure:

1. Start with a short lesson starter activity (e.g. spelling) lasting 10–15 minutes
2. Introduce the main teaching points (e.g. teacher exposition)
3. Develop the main teaching points (e.g. through group activity)
4. End with a plenary to draw out the learning (e.g. through feedback and presentation lasting 5–10 minutes (p. 7)

The framework was essentially a more sophisticated version of the primary literacy framework, emphasizing the skills of: 'spelling, vocabulary, sentence construction, and grammar and style' (DfEE, 2001b, p. 3).

A feature of the implementation of the KS3 Strategy for English was the introduction of six Literacy Progress Units (LPUs) which were targeted at helping pupils in Year 7 who had not achieved level 4 in Year 7. According to the authors of the framework, analysis of KS2 data by QCA indicated that more pupils had difficulties with written tasks compared to reading. Therefore the LPUs were designed to help pupils with these problems and are entitled Writing; Information Retrieval; Spelling; Reading; Phonics and Sentences.

Mathematics
The framework document for Mathematics (DfEE, 2001c) contains a very detailed set of guidelines covering the curriculum in KS3: teaching strategies; inclusion and differentiation; assessment and target setting; and planning. A feature of the KS3 strategy for Mathematics is the recommendation for secondary schools to use a dedicated set of resources called Springboard 7 to help level 3 pupils 'catch up' lost ground over two terms in Year 7.

Science
The emphasis here is to provide a framework (DfES, 2002a) consisting of five key scientific ideas that underpin the Key Stage 3 programme of study: i.e. Cells, Interdependence, Particles, Forces and Energy. This framework contains information about what pupils should know and understand about these key ideas as well as Attainment Target 1 'Scientific Enquiry' in Years 7, 8 and 9.

ICT

The framework for ICT (DfES, 2002c) contains many of the ideas outlined in the documents previously described. It deals with three overarching themes: 'Finding things out; Developing ideas' and 'Exchanging and Sharing information.' Integrated into each of these themes is a further critical feature: Reviewing, modifying and evaluating work as it progresses.

One of the difficulties facing ICT teachers who are trying to implement this strategy is that there is often very little detail passed on from primary schools on the level of attainment of pupils in regard to their ICT skills. In addition, pupils will be developing their skills in other subject areas as appropriate throughout KS3. All this means that, from the ICT subject leader's perspective, monitoring the progress of pupils and assessing their capabilities is particularly challenging at the present time.

The role of subject leaders in the KS3 strategy

According to the DfES (2002d) guidance document, the role is envisaged in three ways:

Judging standards

This means looking carefully at the evidence provided by Key Stage 2 National Tests; baseline data obtained from an analysis of CATs' information when these tests are taken in the first term of Year 7; scrutiny of samples of pupils' work and reviewing the progress of all pupils in Years 7 to 9.

Evaluating the quality of teaching and learning

This involves a detailed consideration of the KS3 schemes of work to ensure they contain sufficient opportunities to enable all pupils to improve. The most suitable forum for discussion of the curriculum is the departmental meeting where there are opportunities for sharing good practice, particularly in the use of starter and plenary activities. Ensuring curriculum continuity between KS2 and KS3 also presents subject leaders with a number of challenges. This is especially true where there are a large of number of feeder primary schools to deal with.

The regular observation of teachers at work in the classroom and subsequent feedback on their teaching presents subject leaders with a number of specific problems. Very often, subject leaders have a full timetable which restricts the actual amount of time available to observe departmental staff. This can be further restricted if a member of the department is absent for any lengthy period of time through stress or illness as work has to be set for the classes not taught. Monitoring the work done by supply teachers can be very time-consuming.

Leading sustainable development

Part of the work of subject leaders centres on the setting of targets for raising pupil attainment which are both challenging and attainable. This is a careful 'balancing act' as the setting of overly ambitious targets will be detrimental to departmental morale. At the same time, less than challenging targets may not win the approval of the SMT or even governors. Raising achievement among the weakest pupils can present Heads of Department with their biggest problem, particularly if they do not have a pool of experienced departmental staff to utilize.

Another part of the job which subject leaders need to do is to identify teaching strategies which might help to improve the quality of pupils' learning and thereby raise attainment. These might include the greater use of starter activities or more time for plenary sessions where pupils engage in self-assessment.

Subject leaders and the implementation of the KS3 strategy

The evidence presented here came from Phase 3 of the research focused on investigating the views of subject leaders working in a variety of different subject areas. The research, in the form of semi-structured interviews, was carried out in three secondary schools (see Appendix 3 for further details) situated in different parts of England in the Summer Term 2003. The comments made by Heads of foundation subjects generally relate to the cross-curricular aspects of the KS3 strategy, particularly in the areas of literacy, numeracy and ICT.

Problems with the implementation of the KS3 strategy

Of the ten subject leaders interviewed in the three sample schools specifically about the KS3 strategy, only five were willing to make any reference to the inevitable problems which arise with the implementation of any change such as this. The Head of History at Woodlands School, who also happened to be the Key Stage 3 Strategy Manager, commented on the overly prescriptive nature of the strategy as it appeared in the advisory documentation from the government Department for Education and Skills (DfES). After some initial problems associated with finding the time to plan lessons in English and Mathematics in line with the strategy, he felt that staff were now more confident about its implementation. He wanted to change the thinking among the staff from uncritical implementation, towards addressing the question 'How can we make it work best for our pupils?'

Several Heads of Department mentioned the 'top-down' pressure to implement the strategy as quickly as possible. For example, the Head of Mathematics in Highway School referred to the time pressures brought about by trying to implement some of the new ideas contained within the Key Stage 3 strategy too quickly. The Head of Science in Highway School noted some problems in giving feedback to the departmental staff, having attended the training for the strategy, as can be seen in these comments:

> I go out on core training and sometimes I will manage to get the school to agree to letting me take someone else from the Faculty. ... Then you come back into school and there is no real opportunity to cascade it properly to the Faculty and it needs to be done quickly ...

The Head of Humanities at Highway School felt that the initial auditing of provision seemed to serve very little purpose, although he acknowledged that the practical approaches contained within the strategy had not yet been fully implemented in his subject.

Implementing specific aspects of the KS3 strategy
Starters and plenaries
In the KS3 strategy, starter activities have tended to be less problematic for teachers to implement than plenaries. This is reflected

in the comments shown below by the Head of History at Woodland School:

> I have my doubts about the idea of a starter for the sake of a starter. It must be very much linked to the learning that's going to go on in the lesson. Some people argue for starters as a warm-up exercise, just to get the kids thinking, but a lot of energy goes into creating a starter just for that purpose. Starters are probably the easiest to start with, for developing the strategy.

The Head of English at Woodland commented on the department's growing awareness of what a plenary session really means and moving away from the notion of a simple summary at the end of a lesson:

> We're just getting to learn about plenaries and what plenary really means. There was an understanding that plenary meant teacher standing up and saying: 'Right this is my plenary; I'm finishing off the lesson. I've now got five minutes to tell you what you've learnt'; that isn't a plenary. A plenary should be an opportunity for students to actually reflect themselves upon what they have learnt and feed it back. There's a whole lot of different ways you can get them to feed it back. As a teacher you can say, I can now move on to my next lesson/my next objective to cover because I'm pretty secure from what they are telling me that they now understand about that particular skill or that particular content.

The Head of History at Woodland School noted that a plenary session should focus on trying to overcome barriers to learning:

> It's become a bit of a myth now that the plenary comes at the end of the lesson, when it could actually come in the middle where it's a chance just for students just to think about how well they are doing. Why have they experienced difficulties? Why has that pupil not experienced difficulties? What are you doing differently that might help that person?

The Head of Science at Highway School felt that the placing of a plenary session was often easier to do in the middle of a lesson because the amount of time available in his school:

the majority of our Key Stage 3 lessons, all bar one lesson in Year 7, are doubles which means that they are 100 minutes long so it is sometimes the case that we have the plenary in the middle.

Expertise in the use of plenaries is growing. The Head of Mathematics at Highway School was very honest in his assessment of their effectiveness:

[A plenary] does fit in quite nicely, apart from the fact that we don't always use it every single lesson.

Interviewer: How long does it normally last?

About five or ten minutes; sometimes it can be just a case of checking have we understood what we've done? It could be just putting a new question on the board and saying: 'What about this question? From what you've learnt today, how would you tackle this one?' We don't always do it; we're not very good at plenaries, we know that as a faculty. We're very good at doing starters and middle bits, but plenaries, we're not quite so good at because that does tend to be the time when you're packing away.

Use of transition units

A good example of the use of transition units came from the Head of Science at Highway School. Although the primary school subject coordinators were not entirely happy with the transition unit or bridging topic, working in this way does attempt to address issues concerning curriculum continuity:

We have a transition unit or a bridging topic; it's the bubbles topic; I don't know if you know it? ... It's looking at different aspects of bubbles. You look at washing up liquid and you blow bubbles; you look at Aero because it's got bubbles in it and you measure bubble volume and that sort of thing. I met with the Key Stage 2 science coordinators this year and they don't like it anymore because there's not enough emphasis on Science 1 in it. We now need to try and put something else in place.

Raising attainment for low achievers

The Head of Mathematics at Highway School demonstrated his awareness of the need to help low-achieving pupils for Year 7.

He described how a specially designed set of resources was used to help those achieving a level 3:

> What we have done is with the very weakest students they are withdrawn and go to learning support. Those on a level 1/level 2 will go to learning support and be taught through them. With the level 3 most of those will go into set 3 and they will have an extra teaching assistant for half of their lessons, so they will have extra support with their actual learning. They've produced 'Springboard 7' resources for us to use which is a folder full of worksheets ... to help get over these key concepts. We used those as another resource to add to our toolkit, but we haven't taken it on hook, line and sinker, because we don't think that's the way to do it and different schools use it in different ways ...

However, when he was asked if it worked, the Head of Mathematics expressed some scepticism and went on to explain why:

> I don't see how you can get all level 3 students up to level 4 in one year, now we're getting extra data on what grade of level 3, so we're getting 3a, 3b, 3c, you do get a bit more information now.

> Interviewer: So 3a is the nearest to 4?

> Yes, so it gives you an idea as to those who are close to a 4 and those are the ones that you could possibly get up to a 4, but my concern is that if you've got a student who's coming in on level 3, they're already having difficulty with their maths anyway if they're level 3. How do you then make them go the whole level in one year when their progression is going to be less than half a level a year? Your average student progresses at half a level a year so how they can jump from a bottom to even just getting into a 4?

Use of booster lessons
The Head of Science at Central School commented very favourably on the use of so-called 'booster' lessons in Year 9, which are designed to help pupils on the level 4/5 boundary achieve a secure level 5 in the National Tests:

> Certainly over the last year they've been good at illustrating the sorts of ways to structure a lesson. I think they're good for

the pupils that they are designed for; it might even be a bit tough for them, but they are certainly challenging enough to try to get pupils up to level 5. They are perhaps not so relevant for level 3 or bottom level 4 pupils. There are some good ideas in there ... it illustrates the sort of thing that the strategy is trying to adopt.

Contributions made by different subjects to cross-curricular skills
These skills include literacy, numeracy and ICT. The Head of Music at Central School gave an interesting example of where specific strategies were being used to develop pupils' literacy skills in his subject:

> We could refer to the literacy target and, as a specific example, say I want you to write down the instructions for what you have to do in this lesson in your planning sheet and then we can look at that and it gives us some sort of idea. This kid has written down what they're supposed to be doing and it's nothing like what I said so it has a number of impacts. Was I speaking clearly enough? Did I try to give too much information in one go for people to be able to take it in?
>
> Other literacy targets might be about spelling key words so in any projects that we do we have certain key words that we want the pupils to understand and be able to spell. Over the course of the year the pupils build up a glossary of key musical terms.

The Head of History at Woodland School had taken a leading role, as the school's KS3 Strategy Manager in its implementation and he was able to provide a detailed insight into current developments regarding cross-curricular aspects of numeracy. Although this work was at an early stage of development, being able to identify common approaches in subjects as diverse as Mathematics, Science, Geography and CDT should help Year 7 pupils develop their skills in this area:

> The person responsible for numeracy across the curriculum is a Mathematics teacher. We decided this year to focus on work in Science, CDT and beginning to look at Geography. So what's happening is conversations are going on between the numeracy coordinator and the Head of Science, Head of CDT, Head of Geography to identify what their needs are and what they want

their students to be able to do in terms of numeracy. The Science department and the Numeracy coordinator have now written a very detailed mapping scheme where they say, for instance, by October we want our Year 7s to read scales. The Mathematics department are now going away with that very detailed scheme to look at how they need to tweak their own schemes of work to help the Science department. It's coming up with common approaches and common language so that students can see instantly that there is a link between what they did earlier in the Mathematics lesson and what they are now doing in Science.

Working with the Key Stage 3 Manager
What emerged from the research evidence was that the KS3 Strategy Manager appeared to be concerned with two key issues: internal consistency in terms of the implementation of the strategy and the allocation of funding. As far as consistency is concerned, it is the nature of the subject itself that will determine the extent to which the framework can be applied universally. For example, plenary sessions can be more difficult to implement in some subjects than in others.

The allocation of funding is particularly important to subject leaders as funding for other kinds of INSET activity was being reduced. This seemed to be an attempt, as a direct result of government funding policies, to channel CPD activity towards the implementation of the KS3 strategy at the expense of other kinds of INSET. The Head of Science at Central School was able to give some insight as to how such monies might be used on obtaining new resources:

When we first heard of the money I went straight to the Key Stage 3 manager and said 'This money is coming in, it's not necessarily intended to be split three ways but let's do that to start with and then we'll see if we need to via money from one department to another', so we've had full access to Key Stage 3 funding . . .

Interviewer: So what's that money been spent on then?

Well, the money comes in under different headings; Year 8 mentoring, Year 9 booster, so we've bought books, revision guides, past exam papers, photocopying of tests and that sort of thing for the Year 9s, and for mentoring we bought some software which is good, including revision software.

Working with LEA consultants
Funding has been available in some LEAs for the creation of localized consultants to assist schools in the implementation of the strategy. Their influence could be a positive factor in helping to introduce it effectively. One example of this process was given by the Head of Mathematics at Highway School:

> We are working with our numeracy consultant from the LEA who is one of the advisory teachers from the LEA. They come in and work with you on the Key Stage 3 strategy, helping with INSET. They have come to observe people, give them ideas, help us with our development plan for the year and review it.

This Head of Mathematics compared the roles of the Key Stage 3 Strategy Manager with the LEA consultant and commented that, because the consultant was a mathematician (an ex-Head of Mathematics), his function was far more useful. He did not think the KS3 Strategy Manager could do that; they have not got the expertise.

Evidence of the impact of the KS3 strategy on standards

There are some early signs that the implementation of the KS3 strategy is having a positive impact on educational standards. The most recently published Ofsted evaluation report (2004) noted that, in 2003, results in National Tests:

> improved most significantly in mathematics and in the proportion of pupils achieving level 6 in science. The number of schools achieving the DfES floor targets in the core subjects also rose significantly in 2003. (p. 3)

This indicates that more pupils are achieving the higher levels in Mathematics and Science but has been less effective with lower-achieving pupils. The Ofsted (2004) report noted some slight improvements in standards in English, especially in the pupils' skills in speaking and listening.

Summary

Arguably, the introduction of the KS3 strategy has given central government more direct control over the way in which teachers approach the process of teaching. Examples of this can be seen in the advocacy of the three or four-part lesson (including starter activities and plenary sessions) and the use of 'booster' lessons with pupils who are deemed to be underachieving. The use of targeted funding for INSET connected to the implementation of the KS3 strategy is a further indication of the way in which this control is being exercised. The publication of a five-year strategy document recently (DfES, 2004) only serves to reinforce the impression that central government wishes to extend this control over the whole of the 11–16 age range. Whether such a course of action is desirable is much more debatable and, in my opinion, it would not be advisable. This is mainly because any extension of the KS3 strategy into KS4 runs the risk of straitjacketing teachers to teach lessons in a particular way which takes no account of the extreme diversity between subjects at GCSE level.

The evidence from this research and from the most recent evaluation of the impact of the KS strategy (Ofsted, 2004) presents a rather mixed picture.

The use of resources targeted for use with pupils not yet achieving level 4 in subject like English and Mathematics in Year 7 has not yet shown any real impact on pupil performance. However, the use of the so-called 'booster' lessons for pupils in Year 9 Science lessons for pupils not yet achieving level 5 does seem to have had some impact on achievement levels.

In some schools, the adoption of transition units between KS2 and KS3 has not been without its problems. Perhaps the most developmental aspect of the KS3 strategy from a subject leader's perspective is the focus on starter activities and plenary sessions. Here there is an opportunity for the whole department in departmental meetings to reflect on what might be good practice at the start of lessons. The use of plenary sessions has proved to be more problematic for subject leaders both to encourage and embed in practice. However, departmental discussion on both starters and plenaries has given opportunities for sharing good practice. A further potential spin-off has been the use of LEA consultants to advise subject leaders about the implementation of the strategy. This has almost inevitably led to further discussions about how to achieve high standards of teaching and learning, as can be illustrated in a recently published Ofsted report (2003). Here the inspectors comment that, in Science:

> The impact of the more effective consultants was apparent in the departments with which they had worked. They provided a stimulus for development. They knew the schools well and provided a range of in-school support tailored to individual needs. Where consultants established development groups for teachers, these were very successful in sharing and disseminating good practice. (p. 15)

While there is some evidence that teaching styles have adapted, there is no substantial evidence to date that it has had any real effect on standards of achievement. The KS3 strategy needs more time to become embedded in the practice of teaching and learning in secondary schools. Only then will more reliable evidence of impact emerge.

Discussion points and practical activities
1. To what extent are the various elements in the Key Stage 3 strategy used in your subject teaching?
2. What help do low-achieving pupils currently receive to help raise their levels of attainment? How might the employment of 'booster' lessons help these pupils?
3. To what extent are plenary sessions conducted as a routine part of lessons in your subject area? How effective are they in helping pupils consolidate their learning? How could their effectiveness be improved?
4. List the benefits to be gained and the potential drawbacks associated with the use of starter activities in both KS3 and KS4.
5. Literacy, numeracy and ICT are all important key skills. How do you judge the work done in your subject contributes to the development of each skill? Use the following scale to make these judgements and complete Table 12.1 below:

	1	2	3
	Very little contribution	Some contribution	A substantial contribution

Table 12.1   Key skills development in my subject area

Key Skill	In Key Stage 3	In Key Stage 4	In Key Stage 5
Literacy			
Numeracy			
ICT			

Further reading

For information about managing the second year of the KS3 Strategy, visit
   http://www.standards.dfes.gov.uk/keystage3/respub/ws_manyear2
For general information about the KS3 Strategy from an LEA perspective, visit www.norfolkesinet.org.uk/pages/viewpage.asp

13 Your role in the bigger picture

Introduction

This concluding chapter examines how subject leaders contribute to the work of the whole school in relation to the ways in which they deal with the part of the 'jigsaw' for which they have responsibility. It takes as an organizing framework the TTA model of subject leadership, using each of the four major areas referred to earlier in Chapter 3 (Table 3.1), as a focus for this discussion. It is interlaced with illustrative comments from the Headteacher of Highway School who describes the expectations of the SMT in terms of what HoDs might do and how they do their job.

However, the first part of this chapter concerns the nature and specifics of the bigger picture which many headteachers would want their subject leaders to be aware of, as well as including a brief discussion of the role of the SL within this bigger picture.

What is the bigger picture?

This is very much concerned with dealing with the wider vision of what the school is about, where it wants to go and trying to enable individual staff to realize their part in fulfilling this vision. In my view, when it comes to considering the bigger picture, it is difficult to disagree with the sentiments expressed in the Education Reform Act (1988) which required all state schools to provide pupils with a curriculum which is balanced and broadly based; promoted their spiritual, moral, cultural, mental and physical development and prepared them for the opportunities, responsibilities and experiences of adult life. The realization of these aims inevitably leads the SMT and governors to establish a number of priorities for the school.

It is the prime responsibility of the Headteacher and the rest of the SMT to ensure that the school priorities are clearly spelt out, for example, at the start of the academic year. Having said that, all headteachers would expect HoDs to 'fight their corner' and argue a coherent and convincing case for timetable space and appropriate resources to enable the subject staff to do their jobs effectively.

What might the role of the subject leader be in this bigger picture?

Developing a more holistic, whole-school perspective is very important for those subject leaders who wish to seek promotion to more senior roles and become part of the SMT themselves. However, as Heads of Department, they need to view the school through bifocal lenses: on the one hand, developing their perception of the needs of the whole school while on the other acting as the main advocate for the needs of their subject. One way of developing a more whole-school role is to volunteer to take charge of a school improvement group which is focused on a whole-school priority, for example, boys' underachievement.

The HoDs have a vital role in helping to create a positive ethos in the department and celebrating success when it is achieved. By developing departmental policies in line with those of the whole school, they can also help to ensure that there is some degree of consistency which pupils can experience when they move from one subject to another.

Strategic direction and development of the subject

Successful subject leaders need to have a clear vision of how they want teaching and learning in the subject to develop. However, to bring about improvements inevitably means being willing to take some risks when introducing changes. In Chapter 6, teacher resistance to change was briefly discussed and the subject leader will have to make some decisions about which change will be given the highest priority in the department. The ability to motivate staff and engender their support through discussion can help to minimize resistance. Most of the time, HoDs are required to implement changes in whole-school policy and create departmental initiatives in line with these changes; for example, in assessment or behaviour. The expectations of the Headteacher can be seen in the following comments:

> I would expect each department to produce their response to the whole-school policy on for example, assessment, or their interpretation of that document with things which are specific to their subject but which reflect the different situations within different departments. So it's important that heads of departments make sure that those policies are not only there, but also are being applied in practice, so your evaluation of the policy and your monitoring of the policy which is every bit as important as writing the policy itself.

However, subject leaders are also required to draw up detailed plans partly to reassure the SMT that the department knows where it is going over the next year and partly to provide a set of agreed goals to which all the members of the department can subscribe.

I suggested in Chapter 7 that there are certain limitations placed on HoDs when it comes to strategic planning. Departmental development plans play a useful role in establishing internal coherence and consistency of approach, provided they are thoroughly discussed and regularly reviewed. Action planning can also help to drive the department forward. As far as the linkages between whole-school and departmental action plans are concerned, the Headteacher commented:

> I'd expect them very clearly to set out what the aim was they were seeking to achieve, the tasks that they plan to perform in order to achieve them, who was going to be primarily responsible for achieving them and who is the link person for that.

Interviewer: So that would be a named person?

> A named person, a time constraint by which the task would be performed, and success criteria. I think success criteria are the most difficult to write because you can tend to get very circular; i.e. you can tend to say we are going to do this and your success criteria is we've done this. You've got to try and make sure you quantify or illustrate the effect that what you have done has had.

For example, it could be for the library; we will increase the number of books which are attractive to boy readers. The success criteria would not be 'we bought those books'; it would be 'we have a greater number of boys reading these books'.

It is essential for subject leaders to monitor the progress being made (at regular intervals) towards the achievement of the goals outlined in the departmental plans. This plays a major part in the ongoing discussions between the line manager and the HoD as well as being discussed in departmental meetings. In this context, the Headteacher noted that:

> I think that it's important that the plan is a working document . . . it should be there as a constant reminder of what you're about or what you're planning to do. Certainly at every departmental meeting there ought to be an item on the agenda which looks at progress on the school development plan, where all members of staff can then discuss progress and say whether there have been any problems that have arisen, are we on course. Every time they meet their line manager then progress on the school development plan should be a key item on the agenda.

Teaching and learning

In the current educational context, there is one overarching theme which applies to the work of HoDs in relation to teaching and learning and that is accountability. There is an expectation on the part of the SMT that pupils in KS3 and KS4 should at the very least be achieving at a level commensurate to their ability which is usually rated on the basis of CATs' scores and performance in KS2. Target grades for the subject will be set for GCSE pupils in Year 10 and it is the responsibility of the HoD to ensure that progress towards these goals is monitored carefully and intervention strategies are used with underperforming pupils. Monitoring teaching and learning can also be carried out within the PM context where lessons would be observed on an annual basis. Line managers may decide to introduce more frequent observations as part of the drive to raise standards.

These targets are quantitative and being able to satisfy the demands of accountability means, for the HoD, that ready access to data becomes very important. In the Headteacher's view:

All heads of department should be aware of what's going on in the classrooms within their department and if they are asked what is the progress of such and such a group, they ought to have some information to hand or be able to get hold of some information to answer that question, so there's regular assessment information they should be holding. They should also have as part of that information the targets that have been set for those students; those targets could perhaps be drawn from NFER cognitive ability tests or they could have been individual targets set by the teachers with reference to those NFER tests. But that information should be available and it's the role of the head of department to make sure that students are achieving commensurate with their ability during Key Stage 3 and during Key Stage 4.

There is also an expectation that different groups of pupils (by age and ability) would be monitored carefully to determine whether any group was underachieving by comparison with their expected levels of achievement. For example:

Interviewer: Would it be possible to pick up whether certain groups were not being monitored closely enough?

Well it would be part of again the discussion with the line manager to say that recent examinations in your subject, what does your analysis show? We do the formal analysis obviously in September when we send a pro forma out to heads of department and they have to respond to some fixed questions and provide a complete analysis of GCSE and A level results. . . . So it's important that heads of department make sure that they know how well pupils are doing.

Any evaluation of teaching and learning will also consider whether the curriculum that is being taught is suited to the range of pupils' abilities. Successful subject leaders will want to encourage the departmental staff to use a range of teaching styles to match the range of preferred learning styles of the pupils.

When it comes to the evaluation of teaching and learning, the expectations of the Headteacher were: 'there will be lesson observations, work sampling and analysis of performance data'. In addition to the requirements for performance management, the Headteacher indicated that staff were observed teaching on one further occasion each year using the Ofsted criteria on the quality of teaching and learning.

One of the key lessons from Chapter 8 is that subjects differ markedly from each other and place emphasis on a range of knowledge and skills unique to the subject itself. Some subjects are dominated by content (e.g. Mathematics) while others are skills-based (e.g. reading, writing, speaking and listening skills in English).

However, there are a range of skills which are applicable across the curriculum, most notably literacy, numeracy and ICT. For many schools, these are likely to be ongoing action points. In Highway school, the Headteacher indicated that his expectations related mainly to the use of sampling pupils' work to investigate the extent to which the development of skills was being addressed.

> We've done a specific work sampling which just looked at the literacy, so the Key Stage 3 strategy manager circulated to the heads of department saying, I want you to take some work in and I want you to look specifically for these aspects of literacy.

Self-evaluation in a departmental context offers HoDs an opportunity to take control of the process provided it is carried out in a robust fashion. It is aimed at providing judgements about the quality of teaching and learning as well as the leadership and management being offered. Information can also be obtained from the pupils and parents about teaching and learning.

As far as HoDs are concerned, self-evaluation information can be obtained from lesson observations, line-management meetings, the use of surveys, formal and informal discussion with parents and pupils, work sampling, analysing performance data, sharing good practice and homework monitoring. The lesson observations can be carried out by the HoD but, as an additional means of sharing good practice, colleagues can be encouraged to observe each other on a regular basis.

An example of the criteria used by HoDs in Highway school, in the work-scanning process is shown in Table 13.1.

If the subject leader is the person designated as a Head of Faculty, then there is a limitation on the extent to which they can directly influence the standards of teaching and learning. The Head of Faculty may lack experience and professional credibility in part

Table 13.1 Work-scanning form (included with permission from Highway School)

Assessment criteria	Very good	Good	Poor	Very poor	No comment
Spellings corrected properly according to the Literacy Policy					
Evidence of the implementation of Literacy Strategy					
Exercise books in good order?					
Underlined titles and dates at the start of each lesson's work					
Work completed and not left undone					
Variety of presentation techniques being employed					
Homework clearly identified in the books					
Homework being set regularly					
Work marked regularly					
Evaluative comments in marking					
Rewards being given					
Use of a consistent grading system					

of the curriculum area for which they are responsible. The responsibility is then delegated to another suitably qualified person to drive through the evaluation of teaching and learning process.

Leading and managing staff

HoDs have to adopt a variety of different roles when exercising leadership in their subject area. Of particular importance are those of team leadership, political leadership, managing performance in the subject and managing change. Being able to manage change either in terms of initiating it to bring about desired outcomes, or being responsible for implementing new whole-school policies is of the most fundamental concern to subject leaders. It usually involves some form of risk and being able to cope with uncertainty.

The push for improvement in standards is relentless, from the government downwards, leading to an educational environment of constant change and turbulence. As is discussed in Chapter 6, teacher resistance is almost inevitable yet managing change is perhaps one of the key indicators of being successful as a subject leader, in the eyes of the SMT particularly.

In Chapter 4, the importance of the HoD acting as a team leader was discussed. This involves being able to act as a good role model and being credible in the eyes of your colleagues in terms of the establishment of high standards of teaching and learning. In addition, effective team leaders also run their departmental meetings in a businesslike fashion, encouraging all staff to contribute to the matters under discussion and valuing their opinions. Levels of motivation can also be sustained when staff are thanked publicly and privately for their contributions to the work of the department.

One of key aspects which HoDs sometimes overlook is that they do not need to do all the work themselves. Being able to delegate responsibilities at a departmental level can help sustain the levels of motivation in some staff. It has to be recognized that this option is not always available, especially in small departments where they may only be one full-time teacher.

When HoDs act as political leaders, the emphasis here is on their work in a liaison role with two different sets of people with differing agendas, i.e. departmental staff and the SMT. Conflicts of interest will occasionally arise, as was discussed in Chapter 5. However, as the demands associated with accountability tend to increase, the potential for increasing amounts of departmental conflict may grow as target setting becomes ever more challenging in the light of ambitious government targets for pupil performance in National Tests and public examinations.

One of the more recent initiatives which subject leaders have to grapple with is that of being a performance manager. Monitoring the standards of teaching and learning by means of lesson observation is a very important part of that process. An HoD may have the responsibility for the PM of up to four departmental staff. It would be expected for the person being observed to provide a lesson plan and any contextual information about the class. After the lesson, the HoD would provide some written feedback setting out what the strengths and areas for development might be. The yearly review (mentioned in Chapter 1) would then give the HoD a chance to discuss with an individual member of staff the extent to which they might have met their targets at a whole-school, departmental and personal level. New targets for the forthcoming year can then be agreed, in the light of current whole-school initiatives and priorities.

The PM process may well uncover training needs for departmental staff which have to be addressed. A key area in the work of an HoD to raise educational standards is to be able to help address the training needs of all departmental staff.

> Well, these are identified as part of performance management, so that is a separate sheet which goes to the professional development coordinator and he or she then maps that into the school provision. Increasingly, we are sending fewer and fewer people out on courses, partly because of the resourcing issue and partly because of workforce reform where teachers cannot be expected to cover for other teachers. Inevitably something has got to go so we're looking at more in-house, much more using training days more productively. (Headteacher, Highway School)

One useful point to be made here is that the HoD may wish to utilize the strengths of other members of the department to lead developments in, for example, ICT.

HoDs will want to create the best possible team in order to be as effective as possible. One way of achieving this is to be involved in the selection of new departmental staff. There are a number of aspects of this process which are important: the drawing up of a person specification and job description giving potential candidates as much information about the current state and intended future of the subject department as possible. It would also be vital to draw up criteria for the interview stage which would help in identifying the best candidate for the post. Time alone with each candidate on the day of the interview would also be very helpful in forming a judgement. Once the successful candidate has been offered and accepted the post, the process of induction for new members begins.

According to the Headteacher of Highway School:

> Their involvement is key, so I would expect them to be involved at every level, so when a post comes up I would expect them to produce some information for candidates, to see what their priorities are, to produce a draft person specification which they'll then talk through with their line manager, to make sure we are all singing from the same song-sheet, but the person has got to work in that department, so I want to make sure that that head of department produces something which is going to attract good staff.

He went on to comment on the selection criteria which might be used, as part of the preparation with the line manager, and to consider the following questions:

> What are we really looking for?
> What are the key attributes?
> What are desirable?
> What are the essential skills needed?

It might also be the case that all candidates for a teaching post actually teach, so it would be expected that the HoD would set up the group to be taught and make other relevant arrangements.

Deployment of staff and resources

This section will discuss some of the issues concerning the management of human resources, financial resources and the learning environment from the HoD perspective. As far as human resources are concerned, successful HoDs will be fully aware of the subject-knowledge background, pedagogical expertise and teaching skills of the departmental staff. Utilizing these strengths to the best effect is challenging in that it requires time to be spent with each member of staff in informal discussion as well as observing them teach in the classroom. In addition, the person responsible for drawing up the timetable should be consulted as discussions need to take place in regard to the effective deployment of the staff available.

Managing financial resources involves two aspects: budgeting and costing. The former is important as the HoD will want to use the available resources as efficiently as possible. The latter relates to the fact that the HoD wants to be putting in a bid to the SMT for additional resources to meet a desired educational objective. Burton (in Brundrett and Terrell, 2004, p. 175) discusses various approaches to costings for the introduction of citizenship schemes by way of an example. He suggests four different sorts of costs need to be borne in mind: initial costs; recurring costs; marginal costs and additional direct costs.

Managing a delegated budget presents all subject leaders with different problems mainly related to the nature of the subject being taught. For example, Heads of English may wish to recommend the purchase of new set of books, while Heads of Science will want to replenish stocks of consumable items. Demands for the financing of new courses can also put pressure on the school's budget, yet the HoD is expected to 'fight their corner' and put together a convincing case to the SMT for the maximum amount of resource to be allocated to their subject. The position taken by the HoD would reflect the outcome of discussions held in departmental meetings.

By way of example, the Headteacher of Highway school emphasized the need for HoDs to be realistic in their bidding for often limited financial resources:

> What we do here is the departments say what they need in order to maintain what they are doing, just to run the department. All those bids come in and we look at it against the budget as an SMT and then decide what the allocation is going to be and I have to say the more that people have done it, the more realistic that they are ... they realise If everyone who plays the game, plays consistently, and is realistic, then you are more likely to get what you need.

Creating an effective learning environment involves both staff and students. It may be possible for the HoD to arrange a regular meeting place for departmental staff which can help foster a positive ethos and nurture teamwork. The HoD has responsibility for safety in the subject area. However, it also involves other significant details, such as seating arrangements for pupils, the layout of the classroom and the quality of the display work around the corridors and in the classrooms. Flexibility is achievable if the tables are mobile, allowing small group discussion to be undertaken more easily.

In terms of the expectations of the Headteacher of an effective learning environment, the following comments relate specifically to lesson observations:

> I think the expectations are that departments are welcoming places. There are good displays on the walls, staff and students feel at ease within them ... the role of the head of department and teachers is to make sure that there are display materials made available so that support staff can put them up. Looking at the level of learning environments as well, I would expect to see round the place, key words; helpful hints about how to get to level 4 instead of level 3; what you need to do to improve; what does a grade C in geography mean? In English, you'd expect to see different words, to see key words around the rooms, so it's make sure those are there; the layout of the room, make sure it's an effective working arrangement, make sure that teachers are using the space properly and that again would be something you'd comment on in lesson observation.

Looking ahead: changes in the role of the subject leader

This final section of the book is devoted to speculating about the effect of various changes might have on the work of subject leaders, especially in the areas of workforce reform and use of ICT.

Workforce reform
In a recent agreement between the government and the majority of the teaching unions, details of which can be found in The School Teachers' Pay and Conditions document (2003) – this can be accessed on the teachernet website, it is recognized that there is a

need to reduce teacher workload and increase the role of support staff in the school. It covers areas such as the allocation of dedicated leadership and management time, which subject leaders need to discharge their responsibilities effectively. However, the agreement does not specify how much time might be available leaving open the question as to whether this will bring about any real improvement in the effectiveness of subject leaders.

From September 2004, the amount of cover provided by an individual teacher cannot exceed 38 hours in an academic year. Once the limit has been reached, the document envisages various options being available for schools to use including supply teachers, higher level teaching assistants, cover supervisors and 'floating teachers'. Undoubtedly, much of the responsibility for managing these staff will be delegated to the HoD which may not ultimately reduce their workload or make them any more effective.

Increasing use made of ICT

The rapidly changing context is worth a brief mention. Personal laptop computers are useful in providing pupils with more independence in their learning. It is quite likely that in future, pupils will be able to access and process information using hand-held devices. These offer even more opportunities for work to be done outside lessons and to be structured so that learners can work at their own pace. This does not have to be driven forward by the subject leader themselves. Recent entrants to the teaching profession now have a far greater range of ICT skills and expertise than their predecessors. According to Kennewell (2004, p. 193):

> ICT-capable subjects have a head of department who is ICT capable and provides appropriate leadership in the use of ICT. There will often be a junior member of the department who has greater specialist knowledge of ICT in the subject and represents the department on the school ICT committee.

Discussion points
1 (a) What are your current school improvement targets?
   (b) When these targets are met, how do you celebrate success and recognize the achievements of the pupils in your subject?

2. How frequently do you, as an HoD, share your ideas about good standards of teaching and learning in departmental meetings?

3 (a) To what extent has your school developed its own self-evaluation policies?

   (b) How useful is the form for work scanning shown in Table 13.1? Is something like this used in your school?

4. How do you think part-time and full-time staff in your department may be deployed more effectively in the light of the recent workforce reforms?

5. (a) Which areas of your work as a subject leader do you think you could improve?

   (b) Share your ideas with your line manager and devise a strategy which will help you improve your own performance in one of those areas of relative weakness.

Further reading

Given that the bigger picture is contextualized in a rapidly changing educational context, I would recommend you read Part 10 'Schools of the Future' edited by Brian Caldwell in Davies, B. and West-Burnham, J. (eds) (2003) *Handbook of Educational Leadership and Management*, Harlow: Pearson Education.

Bowring-Carr, C. and West-Burnham, J. (1997) *Effective Learning in Schools: How to Integrate Learning and Leadership for a Successful School*, London: Financial Times Management, Pitman Publishing.

Field, K., Holden, P. and Lawlor, H. (2000) *Effective Subject Leadership*, London: Routledge.

References

ACCAC (2000) *Mathematics in the National Curriculum in Wales*, Cardiff: ACCAC.

Adair, J. (1987) *Not Bosses but Leaders*, London: Kogan Page.

Adey, K. (2000) 'Professional development priorities: the views of middle managers in secondary schools', *Educational Management and Administration* 28 (4): 419–31.

Adey, K. and Jones, J. (1998) 'Development needs of middle managers: the views of senior managers', *Journal of In-Service Education* 24 (1): 131–44.

Adler, S., Laney, J. and Packer, M. (1993) *Managing Women*, Buckingham: Open University Press.

Arrowsmith, R. (2001) 'A right performance' in Gleeson, D. and Husbands, C. (eds) *The Performing School: Managing Teaching and Learning in a Performance Culture,* London: Routledge.

Ball, S. (1993) *The Micro-Politics of the School: Towards a Theory of School Organisation*, London: Routledge.

Becher, T. (1989) *Academic Tribes and Territories*, Milton Keynes: Open University Press.

Bell, L. and Bawden, A. (2000) *Researching Educational Management and Leadership in Primary Schools in England: The Role of the Head*, Paper for the SCRELM symposium, BEMAS Research Conference, Robinson College, Cambridge University, 29th–30th March.

Bennett, N. (1995) *Managing Professional Teachers: Middle Management in Primary and Secondary Schools*, London: Paul Chapman.

Bennett, N. (1999) 'Middle management in secondary schools: an introduction', *School Leadership and Management* 19 (3): 289–92.

Bennett, N. (2003) *The Role and Purpose of Middle Leaders in Schools*, National College for School Leadership (NCSL) accessible on the following website: www.ncsl.org.uk

Bennett, N., Crawford, M. and Riches, C. (eds) (1992) *Managing Change in Education*, London: Paul Chapman.

Blasé, J. and Anderson, G. (1995) *The Micropolitics of Educational Leadership*, London: Cassell.

Black, P. and Wiliam, D. (2002) *Working inside the Black Box: Assessment for Learning in the Classroom*, London: King's College.

Bolam, R. (1999) 'Educational administration, leadership and management: towards a research agenda' in Bush, T., Bell, L., Bolam, R., Glatter, R. and Ribbins, P. (eds) *Educational Management: Redefining Theory, Policy and Practice*, London: Paul Chapman.

Bolam, R. and Turner, C. (1999) 'The management role of subject department heads in the improvement of teaching and learning' in Bolam, R. and van Wieringen, F. (eds) *Research on Educational Management in Europe*, Berlin: Waxmann.

Bolam, R. and McMahon, A. (2004) 'Recent developments in CPD' in Day, C. and Sachs, J. (eds) *International Handbook of the Continuing Professional Development of Teachers*

Bolman, L. and Deal, T. (1994) 'Looking for leadership: another search party's report', *Educational Administration Quarterly* (30) 1: 77–96.

Bradley, H. (1991) *Staff Development*, London: Falmer Press.

Brown, M. and Rutherford, D. (1998) 'Changing roles and raising standards: new challenges for heads of department', *School Leadership and Management* 18 (1): 75–88.

Brown, M., Rutherford, D. and Boyle, B. (2000) 'Leadership and school improvement: the role of the head of department in UK secondary schools', *School Effectiveness and School Improvement* 11 (2): 237–58.

Brundrett, M. and Terrell, I. (eds) (2004) *Learning to Lead in the Secondary School*, London: Routledge.

Bryman, A. (1999) 'Leadership in organisations' in Clegg, S. R., Hardy, C. and Nord, W. (eds) *Managing Organisations: Current Issues*, London: Sage.

Buchanan, D. and Boddy, D. (1992) *The Expertise of the Change Agent*, Hemel Hempstead: Prentice Hall International.

Burns, J. M. (1978) *Leadership*, New York: Harper Row.

Bush, T. (2003) *Theories of Educational Management*, London: Sage.

Busher, H. and Harris, A. (1999) 'Leadership of school subject areas: tensions and dimensions of managing in the middle', *School Leadership and Management* 19 (3): 305–17.

Busher, H. and Harris, A. (2000) *Subject Leadership and School Improvement* London: Paul Chapman.

Craft, A. (1996) *Continuing Professional Development: A Practical Guide for Teachers and Schools*, London: Routledge.

Day, C. (1997) 'In-service teacher education in Europe: conditions and themes for development in the 21st century', *Journal of In-Service Education* 23 (1): 39–54.

DfEE (2000) *Performance Management in Schools: Performance Management Framework*, London: DfEE.

DfEE (2001a) *KS3 National Strategy: Framework for teaching English: Years 7, 8 and 9*, London: DfEE publications.

DfEE (2001b) *KS3 National Strategy: Framework for teaching English Years 7, 8 and 9: Management Summary*, London: DfEE publications.

DfEE (2001c) *KS3 Strategy Framework for teaching Mathematics: Years 7, 8 and 9*, London: DfEE publications.

DfES (2001) The Standards Site, which can be accessed at: www.standards.dfes.gov.uk/keystage3

DfES (2002a) *KS3 Strategy Framework for teaching Science: Years 7, 8 and 9*, London: DfES publications.

DfES (2002b) *Releasing Potential, Raising Attainment: Managing Data in Secondary Schools,* London: DfES publications.

DfES (2002c) *KS3 Strategy Framework for teaching ICT capability: Years 7, 8 and 9*, London: DfES publications.

DfES (2002d) *KS3 Strategy Framework Securing Improvement: The Role of Subject Leaders*, London: DfES publications.

DfES (2002e) The Autumn Package home page can be accessed at: http://www.standards.dfes.gov.uk/performance/ap/index

DfES (2004) *Five Year Strategy for Children and Learners*, London: HMSO.

Earley, P. (1998) 'Middle management – the key to organisational success?' in Middlewood, D. and Lumby, J. (eds) *Strategic Management in Schools and Colleges*, London: Paul Chapman.

Earley, P. and Fletcher-Campbell, F. (1992) *Time to Manage*, Slough: NFER/Nelson.

Eraut, M. (1994) *Developing Professional Knowledge and Competence,* London: Falmer Press.

Estyn (1999) *How well are we doing? A survey of self-evaluation in secondary schools*, Cardiff: Estyn.

Everard, K. B., Morris, G. and Wilson, I. (2004) *Effective School Management*, London: Paul Chapman.

Fidler, B. (1997) 'Strategic Management', in Fidler, B., Russell, S. and Simkins, T. (eds) *Choices for Self-Managing Schools: Autonomy and Accountability*, London: Paul Chapman.

Field, K., Holden, P. and Lawlor, H. (2000) *Effective Subject Leadership*, London: Routledge.

Fleming, P. (2000) *The Art of Middle Management in Secondary Schools*, London: David Fulton.

Fullan, M. (1993) *Change Forces: Probing the Depths of Educational Reform*, London: Falmer Press.

Fullan, M. (1999) *Change Forces: The Sequel*, London: Falmer Press.

Fullan, M. (2003) *Change Forces with a Vengeance*, London: RoutledgeFalmer.

Galton, M., Gray, J. and Ruddock, J. (1999) *The Impact of School Transitions and Transfers on Pupil Progress and Attainment*, Research Report No. 131. London: Department for Education and Employment.

Galton, M., Gray, J. and Ruddock, J. (2003) *Transfer and Transitions in the Middle Years of Schooling (7–14): Continuities and Discontinuities in Learning*, Research Report No. 443.

Gardner, H. (1993) *Multiple Intelligences: The Theory in Practice*, New York: Basic Books.

General Teaching Council for Wales (2002) *Continuing Professional Development: An Entitlement for All, The General Teaching Council for Wales Draft Advice to the National Assembly for Wales*, Cardiff: GTCW.

General Teaching Council for Wales (2003*) Professional Development Projects Information Booklet 2003–2004*, Cardiff: GTCW.

Glover, D., Gleeson, D., Gough, G. and Johnson, M. (1998) 'The meaning of management', *Educational Management and Administration* 26 (3): 279–92.

Glover, D. and Miller, D., with Gambling, M., Gough, G. and Johnson, M. (1999a) 'As others see us: senior management and subject staff perceptions of the work effectiveness of subject leaders in secondary schools', *School Leadership and Management* 19 (3): 331–44.

Glover, D. and Miller, D, (1999b) 'The working day of the subject leader and the impact of interruptions on teaching and learning in secondary schools', *Research in Education* 62: 55–65.

Gold, A. (1998) *Head of Department: Principles in Practice*, London: Cassell.

Greenfield, T. B. (1986) 'Leaders and schools: wilfulness and non-natural order in organisations' in Sergiovanni, T. J. and Corbally, J. E. (eds) *Leadership and Organisational Culture: New Perspectives on Administrative Theory and Practice*, Urbana and Chicago: University of Chicago Press.

Gronn, P. (2000) 'Distributed properties: a new architecture for leadership', *Educational Management and Administration* 28 (3): 317–38.

Gunter, H. M. (2001) *Leaders and Leadership in Education*, London: Paul Chapman.

Hall, V. (1996) *Dancing on the Ceiling: A Study of Women Managers in Education*, London: Paul Chapman.

Hall, V. (1999) 'Gender and education management' in Bush, T., Bell, L., Bolam, R., Glatter, R. and Ribbins, P. *Educational Management: Redefining Theory, Policy and Practice*, London: Paul Chapman.

Hammond, P. (1998) 'How can a head of department affect the quality of teaching and learning?', unpublished TTA teacher-researcher grant project report.

Hargreaves, A. (1992) 'Contrived collegiality: the micropolitics of teacher collaboration' in Bennett, N., Crawford, M. and Riches, C. *Managing Change in Education*, London: Paul Chapman.

Harland, J. and Kinder, K. (1997) 'Teachers' continuing professional development; framing a model of outcomes', *British Journal of In-service Education* 23 (1): 71–84.

Harris, A. (1998) 'Improving ineffective departments in secondary schools', *Educational Management and Administration* 26 (3): 269–78.

Harris, A. (2001) 'Building the capacity for school improvement', *School Leadership and Management* 21 (3): 261–70.

Harris, A., Jamieson, I. and Russ, J. (1997) 'A study of effective departments in secondary schools' in Harris, A., Bennett, N. and Preedy, M. (eds) *Organisational Effectiveness and Improvement in Education*, Buckingham: Open University Press.

Hart, A. W. and Weindling, D. (1996) 'Developing successful leaders' in Leithwood, K., Chapman, J., Corson, D., Hallinger, P. and Hart, A. (eds) *International Handbook of Educational Leadership and Administration*, Boston: Kluwer Academic.

Hartle, F., Everall, K. and Baker, C. (2001) *Getting the best out of Performance Management in your School*, London: Kogan Page.

Helsby, G. and McCulloch, G. (1997) *Teachers and the National Curriculum*, London: Cassell.

Hersey, P., Blanchard, K. and Johnson, D. (1996) *Management of Organisational Behaviour: Utilising Human Resources*, Englewood Cliffs, NJ: Prentice-Hall.

Hodgkinson, C. (1991) *Educational Leadership – The Moral Art*, Albany, NY: State University of New York Press.

Hopkins, D. and Harris, A. (2000) *Creating the Conditions for Teaching and Learning*, London: David Fulton.

Hoyle, E. (1982) 'Micropolitics of educational organisations', *Educational Management and Administration* 10: 87–98.

Hoyle, E. (1986) *The Politics of School Management*, London: Hodder & Stoughton.

Hughes, M. (1987) 'Leadership in professionally staffed organisations' in Hughes, M., Ribbins, P. and Thomas, H. (eds) *Managing Education: The System and the Institution*, London: Cassell.

James, C. and Connolly, U. (2000) *Effective Change in Schools*, London: Routledge.

Joyce, B., Calhoun, E. and Hopkins, D. (1999) *The New Structure of School Improvement: Inquiring Schools and Achieving Students* Buckingham: Open University Press.

Joyce, B. and Showers, B. (1988) *Student Achievement through Staff Development*, New York: Longman.

Katz, N. H. and Lawyer, J. W. (1994) *Preventing and Managing Conflict in Schools*, Thousand Oaks, CA: Corwin Press.

Katzenbach, J. R. and Smith, D. K. (1993) *The Wisdom of Teams: Creating the High Performance Organisation*, Boston, MA: Harvard Business School Press.

Kennewell, S. (2004) *Meeting the Standards in using ICT for Secondary Teaching*, London: RoutledgeFalmer.

Leithwood, K., Begley, P. T. and Cousins, J. B. (1994) *Developing Expert Leaders for Future Schools*, London: Falmer Press.

Lumby, J. (2003) 'Vision and strategic planning' in Bush, T. and Bell, L. (eds) *The Principles and Practice of Educational Management*, London: Paul Chapman.

Luthans, F. (1998) *Organisational Behaviour*, Boston, MA: Irwin McGraw-Hill.

Marland, M. and Hill, S. (1981) *Departmental Management*, London: Heinemann.

Maynard, T. (2002) *Boys and Literacy: Exploring the Issues*, London: Routledge.

Mintzberg, H. (1990) 'The manager's job: folklore and fact', *Harvard Business Review*, March–April: 163–76.

Morrison, K. (1998) *Management Theories for Educational Change*, London: Paul Chapman.

Myers, K. (1996) *TES School Management Update*, 29 November, 6.

Neil, P. and Morgan, C. (2003) *Continuing Professional Development for Teachers*, London: Kogan Page.

Ofsted (2002) *Good Teaching, Effective Departments*, London: Ofsted Publications Centre.

Ofsted (2003) *The Key Stage 3 Strategy: Evaluation of the Second Year*, HMI 518, London: Ofsted Publications Centre.

Ofsted (2004) *The Key Stage 3 Strategy: Evaluation of the Third Year*, HMI 2090, London, Ofsted Publications Centre.

OHMCI (1996) *Success in Secondary Schools*, Cardiff: OHMCI.

Oldroyd, D. and Hall, V. (1991) *Managing Staff Development: A Handbook for Secondary Schools*, London: Paul Chapman.

O'Neill, J. (1997) 'Managing through teams' in Bush, T. and Middlewood, D. (eds) *Managing People in Education*, London: Paul Chapman.

O'Neill, J. (2000) 'So that I can more or less get them to do things they really don't want to. Capturing the situated complexities of the secondary school head of department', *Journal of Educational Enquiry* 1 (1): 13–33.

Paechter, C. (2000) *Changing School Subjects: Power, Gender and Curriculum*, Buckingham: Open University Press.

Reber, A. (1993) *Implicit Learning and Tacit Knowledge*, New York: Oxford University Press.

Reeves, J., McCall, J. and MacGilchrist, B. (2001) 'Change leadership: planning conceptualisation and perception' in MacBeath, J. and Mortimore, P. (eds) *Improving School Effectiveness*, Buckingham: Open University Press.

Rhodes, C. and Beneicke, S. (2003) 'Coaching, mentoring and peer-networking: challenges for the management of teacher professional development in schools', *Journal of In-Service Education* 28 (2): 297–309.

Rudd, P. and Davies, D. (2002) *A Revolution in the use of data? The LEA role in data collection, analysis and use and its impact on pupil performance*, Slough: National Foundation for Educational Research.

Sammons, P., Thomas, S. and Mortimore, P. (1997) *Forging Links: Effective Schools and Effective Departments*, London: Paul Chapman.

Schmuck, R. A. and Runkel P. J. (1994) *The Handbook of Organisation Development in Schools and Colleges*, Prospect Heights, IL: Waveland Press.

Schon, D. (1983) *The Reflective Practitioner: How Professionals Think in Action*, London: Maurice Temple-Smith.

Shakeshaft, C. (1987) *Women in Educational Administration*, Newbury Park, CA: Sage.

Siskin, L. S. (1994) *Realms of Knowledge: Academic Departments in Secondary Schools*, London: Falmer Press.

Starratt, R. J. (1995) *Leaders with Vision: The Quest for School Renewal*, Thousand Oaks, CA: Corwin Press.

Stogdill, R. M. (1950) 'Leadership, membership and organisation', *Psychological Bulletin* 47.

Teacher Training Agency (1998) *National Standards for Subject Leaders*, London: TTA.

The School Teachers Pay and Conditions Document (2003) http://www.teachernet.gov.uk/paysite/section4.cfm

Tomlinson, H. (1998) 'Coaching the team', *Managing Schools Today*: 35–7.

Torrington, D. and Weightman J. (1990) *The Reality of School Management*, Oxford: Blackwell.

Turner, C. K. (2000) 'Learning about leading a subject department in secondary schools: some empirical evidence', *School Leadership and Management* 20 (3): 299–313.

Turner, C. K. (2002) 'Subject heads of department in secondary schools in Wales: improving the standards of teaching and learning', unpublished PhD thesis, Cardiff: School of Social Sciences, University of Wales, Cardiff.

Turner, C. K. and Bolam, R. (1998) 'Analysing the role of the subject head of department in secondary schools in England and Wales: towards a theoretical framework', *School Leadership and Management* 18 (3): 373–88.

Wallace, M. (1991) *School-Centred Management Training*, London: Paul Chapman.

Wallace, M. and Hall, V. (1993) *Senior Management Teams in Action*, London: Paul Chapman.

Wallace, M. and Hall, V. (1994) *Inside the SMT: Teamwork in Secondary School Management*, London: Paul Chapman.

Walton, R. E. (1997) 'Managing conflict in organisations' in Crawford, M., Kydd, L. and Riches, C. (eds) *Leadership and Teams in Educational Management*, Buckingham: Open University Press.

Whittaker, P. (1993) *Managing Change in Schools*, Buckingham: Open University Press.

Wise, C. (2000) 'Being a curriculum leader: Helping colleagues to improve learning' in Busher, H. and Harris, A. (eds) *Subject Leadership and School Improvement* London: Paul Chapman.

Wise, C. and Bush, T. (1999) 'From teacher to manager: the role of the academic middle manager in secondary schools', *Educational Research* 41 (2): 183–95.

Wise, C. and Busher, H. (2001) 'The subject leader' in Middlewood, D. and Burton, N. (eds) *Managing the Curriculum*, London: Paul Chapman.

Yukl, G. (1994) *Leadership in Organisations* (3rd edn), Englewood Cliffs, NJ, Prentice-Hall.

Appendix 1
Details of Phase 1 survey

A total of 788 questionnaires were sent to all English-medium and bilingual secondary schools in Wales in 1995. A copy of the survey was sent to the Heads of Science, Technology, English and Mathematics in each school with a covering letter explaining the purposes of the research. 204 responses were received from HoDs, giving a response rate of 26 per cent. The sample of HoDs included representatives from every Welsh Local Education Authority (LEA).

This sample can be broken down as follows:

59 Heads of Science
47 Heads of Technology
54 Heads of English
44 Heads of Mathematics

The overall gender balance in the sample was as follows:

133 (65 per cent) male HoDs
71 (35 per cent) female HoDs

The HoDs were very experienced teachers with the average length of time in teaching being 21 years and the average length of time in post being eight years.

Appendix 2
Details of the Phase 2 research

It was originally intended to interview a total of 40 HoDs in 1997 and 1998, working in ten secondary schools in Wales. In the event, several HoDs were unavailable to be interviewed and the sample size was reduced to 36 HoDs. This sample was made up of nine Heads of English, nine Heads of Mathematics, eight Heads of Technology, and ten Heads of Science. The schools were selected to be representative of HoDs working in large and small schools; situated in rural and urban locations; and located in a variety of LEAs.

Of the 36 HoDs interviewed, 22 (60 per cent) were male and 14 (40 per cent) were female.

Appendix 3
Details of Phase 3 of the research

In 2003, a number of HoDs were interviewed in three secondary schools in England. Six were interviewed in Highway School, working in the following subjects: Vocational Studies; Technology; Mathematics; Modern Languages; Science and Geography. Four HoDs were interviewed in Central School and the HoDs there worked in Mathematics, Music, English and Science. Finally, six HoDs were interviewed in Woodland School and they were responsible for History, English, Business Studies, Personal and Social Education (PSE), Physical Education (PE), and Information and Communications Technology (ICT).

Index